Learning to Believe Again

Learning
to Believe
Again

30 DAYS to Finding Hope, Faith, and Comfort in God's Truth

BRITTANY BEXTON

NASHVILLE

NEW YORK • LONDON • MELBOURNE • VANCOUVER

Learning to Believe Again

30 Days to Finding Hope, Faith, and Comfort in God's Truth

Published in New York, New York, by Morgan James Publishing. Morgan James is a trademark of Morgan James, LLC. www.MorganJamesPublishing.com

ISBN 9781642795226 paperback
ISBN 9781642795233 eBook
Library of Congress Control Number: 2019936258

Cover Design by:
Rachel Lopez
www.r2cdesign.com

Interior Design by:
Chris Treccani
www.3dogcreative.net

Morgan James is a proud partner of Habitat for Humanity Peninsula and Greater Williamsburg. Partners in building since 2006.

Get involved today! Visit
MorganJamesPublishing.com/giving-back

Table of Contents

Introduction

few years ago, I went through one of the hardest experiences of my life. It blew up in a moment and ripped the rug out from under me, but the hurt and discovery came in layers of pain. I lost my faith. I didn't just lose my faith in God. I lost my faith in myself, and in other people. I was broken. I have been a Christian for as long as I can remember. Even when I was a little girl, I poured through the Bible, and prayed every night. When I spoke to God, it wasn't a one-sided narrative; it was a conversation. I could feel God walk with me. I could hear Him speak to me. He led me, He gave me signs, He encouraged my heart. My relationship with God was so real and so close that I could never have questioned His existence. Even after I went through this trial, I still *believed* in God, but I started to wonder if this God that I knew really cared for me, really protected me, and really wanted good things for me. I couldn't understand how God had allowed that to happen to me. I couldn't understand how He could have led me down a path to so much pain. I have lived a life full of trials. But I have also lived through overcoming them. But, when my life exploded, it was just too much. The unresolved pain of years of ungrieved losses had hit its max capacity, and a part of me shut down. I didn't stop believing in God, and I didn't stop praying, but my prayers felt empty, numb, and hopeless. So, I focused on other things, I numbed out the pain, and I did the best I could to survive. I was simply going through the motions.

Then, one night, I met someone who enlivened my spirit again. They reminded me who I am. They reminded me of the vibrancy inside of me that I'd been dulling so I didn't have to hurt. And, they were so full of the love and light of God that it radiated out of them. They reminded me how good it felt to have faith like that. They reminded me how amazing it felt to feel, and trust, and love, and believe in God's goodness. They gave me hope, and they gave me a reason to heal. They woke my spirit up … but that also means they woke up the pain inside me that hadn't been healed. I realized I had PTSD and that I needed to heal. I began my own journey of healing, and through that process, learning to believe again.

That journey meant fighting through hurt and crying years of un-cried tears. It meant digging deeper into God's word. It meant digging into not just the feel-good verses that most people like to preach about but digging into the grittier verses. The verses that spoke more truth about where I was and what I had gone through. The verses that discuss trauma, and pain, and evil. But most of all, the verses that express God's unfailing love, through even the hardest, deepest trials, the biggest betrayals, and even through our mistakes and misinterpretations. But in the pain—through the tears and in the hard verses—I found joy, I found love, I found acceptance, and I found freedom. A freedom that I always knew I was supposed to have with Christ, but had never known.

This devotional is pulled from my own journey to find healing and wholeness with God's word. It's the undoing of years of false beliefs and the bad habit of shutting down my spirit. I replaced those false beliefs and fears with God's truth and God's word. It's my journey back into hope, from broken faith to a belief that I could still have love, and happiness, and good things. I hope in reading this devotional, and studying the word, that you too come to know how loved you are by

God, how precious you are to Him, and that you are worthy of good things. I hope you come to believe that not only are you worthy, but that the very heart of God desires good for you.

Day 1:

I Believe! Help My Unbelief

There are times in life when brokenness doesn't begin to cover how we are feeling. Broken, bruised, drenched, wrung out, cried out, exhausted, depressed, drained, and defeated may be a better description. There are things in life that no matter how strong you are, or how much you love the Lord, they just knock the wind out of you. They are the things you can't plan for. The things you don't expect. The things you never could have imagined. The moments when the rug is pulled out from under your life and, suddenly, nothing looks the way it did, and the things you have built are shaken—but not as shaken as your heart. These traumas can come in all shapes and sizes. Sometimes these events come as illness. Sometimes, they come as a natural disaster. Sometimes, they come as a financial disaster. Sometimes, they come as death or an accident. But perhaps the most shocking and painful is when they come in the form of harm from people who we believed we could trust. It is a painful moment when you realize that someone you love deeply and trust is not who you believed they were. It is hard to trust yourself, or God, or the world, when something as holy and beautiful as love is twisted into something it was never meant to be: abuse, betrayal, fraud. In moments when your entire world looks different, and you are shaken to the core, it can be hard to believe or trust in anything or anyone.

It's hard to trust yourself and your own judgment, it's hard to trust God when you believe He could have prevented the disaster, and it can be extremely hard to trust anyone else. I have been there. I have been in the darkest of places, where everything I believed about my life was turned upside down. Where the ones I loved betrayed me, lied to me, and worst of all, committed fraud against my heart. I had always trusted myself and my judgment until that moment. How could I have been deceived? I had always believed in God, and believed He was for me and protected me, but I didn't feel protected. And I had always believed the best of people. I was careful whom I kept close, but I didn't see evil in people, I saw brokenness and love. So, there I sat: broken, betrayed, harmed, and shaken to the absolute core of my faith, my belief, my being. How could the God I loved so much and trusted so deeply have allowed this to happen to me? Why did He not protect me?

You see, I never even for a moment stopped believing in God. My relationship with God was far too real to ever believe He didn't exist. But, in that dark place where my world and heart were turned upside down, I felt betrayed by God. I believed in Him, but I struggled to believe that He would protect me or give me good things—the desires of my heart. I knew that the Scriptures said that He works all things together for our good and that if we delight in Him, He will give us the desires of our hearts. (Psalm 37:4). I knew that in Jeremiah 29:11 it says He has plans to prosper us, and not to harm us. Plans to give us a future, and a hope. I knew I had seen God work in the lives of others, and even for me at times. But when I looked at the rubble of my life in front of me, and I looked back on the scattered traumas and pains in my past, it was really hard to believe that He would do good things for me.

I would get on my knees every morning and every night and pray as I had always prayed, but these prayers felt empty. I went through the motions, but I felt numb. My heart was numb because it couldn't take any more pain. My mind told me to be safe and just settle for less than what I really wanted, because it was safer. If I settled, I couldn't be hurt the same way again, and I struggled to believe that God would truly come through for me. I had been in pain for so long, and this time, it cut so deeply that hoping for the things I really wanted almost hurt. So, I settled for happy enough. I settled for safe. I settled for content enough. But God didn't. God would not settle for me. God could not settle for me. And, God would not allow me to settle for less than He has for me. You see, while our faith may fail, God remains faithful. (2 Tim. 2:13) Where our hope may fail, God remains faithful to His promises. God can't lie. All of His promises are true. He answers our prayers with "yes" and "amen." And even when we can't feel His presence, He is there. You see, even though the mountains may be shaken, and the hills removed, God's unfailing love for us will not be shaken, and his covenant of peace and blessing to us, will not be removed. (Isaiah 54:10). God is with us and He is for us, no matter how we feel. God proved this faithfulness to me when He brought a person into my life who radiated the light of His love—a person who was so full of God, who loved God and people so much, and had such fervor for life that he reminded me what it felt like to have hope and faith and to trust God. That night, I saw God's light in him, and I remembered what it felt like to have that hope and light in me. And I wanted it back. I began to pray that God would revive His spirit within me and give me my faith and trust back. I leaned into God and sought Him, no matter how hard it was.

Belief still wasn't easy. I was broken. I could see good again, but it was so hard to believe that I could have that good in my own life. It was hard to believe that God would come through for me. I started to see God's favor in my life again, but because of the trauma, it was hard to believe that it would last. I was terrified of losing everything again. It was hard to believe that God would complete the good things He had started in my life (Phil. 1:6). But I desperately wanted to believe. I wanted the blessing. I wanted the breakthrough. I wanted the blessings to last and be built on a healthy and firm foundation. I wanted so badly to believe that these things were possible. So, I got down on my knees and I prayed the only prayer I could pray in full truth: God I believe! Help me overcome my unbelief! (Mark 9:24) Every day I would pray for the desires of my heart, for good, and every day, I would pray, "I believe, God I believe this is possible! I believe you have good things for my future! Help my unbelief!" Slowly but surely, God began to strengthen my faith again. He started speaking to me again. I started to feel His presence again. I still struggled with fear, but I could see the light as well. And God started giving me a new perspective—a higher perspective— on my pain and what I'd gone through. God began to reveal to me the ways that He had tried to speak to me leading up to the collapse. I remembered whispers of warning in my gut. I also started to see the ways in which God was using my past pain to help others and even myself. But, most importantly, He started giving me hope for my future. You see, God works all things together for our good (Rom. 8:28). This means He works with our traumas, our brokenness, and even our own failures and mistakes. He can still use even those painful things for good!

I don't know what you are walking through today. I don't know what your past traumas or pains look like. They may have been caused by mistakes in your life, or they may have been completely out of your control. It is not promised that we will not face hardship in this life. We have an enemy, and the devil loves to attack us and mislead us. But what we are promised is that no weapon formed against us will succeed. (Isaiah 54:17). We are promised that God takes what people, or the devil, intended for our harm, and He uses it for our Good. (Gen. 50:20). And we are promised that God will never leave us or forsake us.

(Deut. 31:6). Nothing can "separate us from the love of God" (Romans 8:38). So, no matter what it is you walk through today, know that God is with you. He is fighting for you. He will not settle, He will not falter, He remains faithful, and He will complete the good work He's started in you. Cry out and ask God to help you believe.

Reference Verses

Genesis 50:20
You intended to harm me, but God intended it all for good. He brought me to this position so I could save the lives of many people.

Deuteronomy 31:6
So be strong and courageous! Do not be afraid and do not panic before them. For the Lord your God will personally go ahead of you. He will neither fail you nor abandon you.

Isaiah 54:10
"For the mountains may move and the hills disappear, but even then my faithful love for you will remain. My covenant of blessing will never be broken," says the Lord, who has mercy on you.

Isaiah 54:15-17
If any nation comes to fight you, it is not because I sent them. Whoever attacks you will go down in defeat. "I have created the blacksmith who fans the coals beneath the forge and makes the weapons of destruction. And I have created the armies that destroy. But in that coming day no weapon turned against you will succeed. You will silence every voice raised up to accuse you. These benefits are enjoyed by the servants of the Lord; their vindication will come from me. I, the Lord, have spoken!"

Jeremiah 29:11-14

"For I know the plans I have for you," says the Lord. "They are plans for good and not for disaster, to give you a future and a hope. In those days when you pray, I will listen. If you look for me wholeheartedly, you will find me. I will be found by you," says the Lord. "I will end your captivity and restore your fortunes. I will gather you out of the nations where I sent you and will bring you home again to your own land."

Psalm 37:1-4

Don't worry about the wicked or envy those who do wrong. For like grass, they soon fade away. Like spring flowers, they soon wither. Trust in the Lord and do good. Then you will live safely in the land and prosper. Take delight in the Lord, and he will give you your heart's desires.

Hebrews 10:22-25

Let us hold tightly without wavering to the hope we affirm, for God can be trusted to keep his promise.

Philippians 1:6

And I am certain that God, who began the good work within you, will continue his work until it is finally finished on the day when Christ Jesus returns.

Mark 9:23-24

"What do you mean, 'If I can'?" Jesus asked. "Anything is possible if a person believes." The father instantly cried out, "I do believe, but help me overcome my unbelief!"

Romans 8:28

And we know that God causes everything to work together for the good of those who love God and are called according to his purpose for them.

Romans 8:38-39

And I am convinced that nothing can ever separate us from God's love. Neither death nor life, neither angels nor demons, neither our fears for today nor our worries about tomorrow—not even the powers of hell can separate us from God's love.

2 Timothy 2:13

If we are unfaithful, he remains faithful, for he cannot deny who he is.

2 Thessalonians 3:2-3

Pray, too, that we will be rescued from wicked and evil people, for not everyone is a believer. But the Lord is faithful; he will strengthen you and guard you from the evil one.

Journal Space

_____

_____

_____

_____

_____

_____

Day 2:

God as an Umbrella

There are times in life when you feel drenched. When the weight of sorrow, grief, fear, and life is just pouring down on you. They say when it rains it pours, but you want to say: Really? Really God? Why? Why another thing? I've had enough! There are times when it doesn't just feel like a torrential downpour, it feels like a bucket has just turned upside down on you. You are waterlogged, and there's no sign of the rain stopping. When you are feeling drenched, it can be hard to believe that the sun will come out, and even harder to look for a rainbow in the mess of the storm, but this is what we're called to. Storms are inevitable; they are a part of life. But we can deal with them in different ways. We can stand outside in the rain being drenched to the core, feeling helpless, or we can grab an umbrella, put on some rain boots, go splash in the puddles, and look for the rainbow! I'm not saying that you should try to just be strong or ignore your feelings—quite the opposite. When you grab an umbrella, you aren't pretending that the rain is not coming down. You are seeing it, hearing it, acknowledging it, and then facing it with all the tools that you have and with a spirit that is looking for the beauty that can come even from the storm.

It's not in our own strength that we face the truth. We can't shelter ourselves from the rain, but God is an umbrella. When you lean into Him, and the hope that there is in Him, you find shelter from the storm, you begin to dry out a bit, and you are able to look at the storm from a new perspective—a perspective of shelter. The water is no longer dripping down into your eyes and blurring your vision. You see the storm with more clarity; you have the sight to look for the rainbow and wait for the sun, knowing that while storms are inevitable, an end to the storm and the sun coming out are also inevitable.

When we stand out in the storm without an umbrella, all we can see and feel is the downpour. And when we try to look back for hope, we don't see the sun, we see the past storms. What we really need to look for is the rainbow in the storm. Because the rainbow is the sign that God is still working and the sunshine is coming. When you are tired and feel waterlogged, you don't need to be strong, and you don't have to ignore the storm. Seek shelter in the One with the umbrella.

Reference Verses

Isaiah 4:6
It will be a shelter from daytime heat and a hiding place from storms and rain.

Isaiah 25:4-5
But you are a tower of refuge to the poor, O Lord, a tower of refuge to the needy in distress. You are a refuge from the storm and a shelter from the heat. For the oppressive acts of ruthless people are like a storm beating against a wall, or like the relentless heat of the desert. But you silence the roar of foreign nations. As the shade of a cloud cools relentless heat, so the boastful songs of ruthless people are stilled.

Isaiah 54:11

O storm-battered city, troubled and desolate! I will rebuild you with precious jewels and make your foundations from lapis lazuli.

Psalm 9:9

The Lord is a shelter for the oppressed, a refuge in times of trouble.

Psalm 31:20

You hide them in the shelter of your presence, safe from those who conspire against them. You shelter them in your presence, far from accusing tongues.

Psalm 91

Those who live in the shelter of the Most High will find rest in the shadow of the Almighty. This I declare about the Lord: He alone is my refuge, my place of safety; he is my God, and I trust him. For he will rescue you from every trap and protect you from deadly disease. He will cover you with his feathers. He will shelter you with his wings. His faithful promises are your armor and protection. Do not be afraid of the terrors of the night, nor the arrow that flies in the day. Do not dread the disease that stalks in darkness, nor the disaster that strikes at midday. Though a thousand fall at your side, though ten thousand are dying around you, these evils will not touch you. Just open your eyes, and see how the wicked are punished. If you make the Lord your refuge, if you make the Most High your shelter, no evil will conquer you; no plague will come near your home. For he will order his angels to protect you wherever you go. They will hold you up with their hands so you won't even hurt your foot on a stone. You will trample upon lions and cobras; you will crush fierce lions and serpents under your feet! The Lord says, "I will rescue those who love me. I will protect those who trust in my name. When they call on me, I will answer; I will be with them in trouble. I will rescue and honor them. I will reward them with a long life and give them my salvation."

Matthew 8:24-26

Suddenly, a fierce storm struck the lake, with waves breaking into the boat. But Jesus was sleeping. The disciples went and woke him up, shouting, "Lord, save us! We're going to drown!" Jesus responded, "Why are you afraid? You have so little faith!" Then he got up and rebuked the wind and waves, and suddenly there was a great calm. (See also Mark 4:35-39)

Journal Space

_____

_____

_____

_____

_____

_____

Day 3:

Brokenness

If we were to be honest, I think we could all say we are broken, or have been broken. And yet, admitting to brokenness, admitting to weakness, admitting to failure, tends to bring up all sorts of shame for most people. But what if brokenness is not something to fear, or hide, or be ashamed of? What if it is the very thing that makes us beautiful? I hid my brokenness for a long time. I pushed back my tears, I never asked for help. I painted on a smile and pretended I had everything together. Deep down I was so scared that if people saw the truth, they would think I was too much. I was scared that I'd be rejected if my vulnerability and weaknesses showed. So, I shut down my hurt and pretended. I desperately wanted to build healthy, loving relationships. I desperately wanted to be accepted, but I wouldn't show anyone the full truth of who I was, so they had no way to accept me—the whole me. I was scared that if people saw my broken pieces, they would run in the other direction, or throw me out like a broken appliance that becomes useless. But our brokenness is different. Our brokenness doesn't render us useless; it forces us to grow and make changes in our lives to heal. Brokenness forces us to have faith to take the next step when we cannot see the whole staircase. Brokenness gives us compassion and the ability to love unconditionally. Brokenness gives us the ability to be seen—fully seen—and accepted. Brokenness creates vulnerability, beautiful open, unabashed vulnerability, and God uses our vulnerability for good.

I like going on walks at dusk. Dusk seems like a magical time, where, for a moment, the whole world quiets down and nature sings. The crickets and frogs sing a sweet lullaby, and the fireflies come out to dance. Soft porch lanterns light up to create a warm and inviting glow. It's like a fairytale world if only for a couple of hours. Dusk is a perfect illustration of the way God uses brokenness in us to make us shine his light far brighter. At dusk, the whole world begins to go dark. The sun goes down and the world gets progressively darker; yet, it is in this darkness that fireflies glow. They light up like an emblem of hope and majesty, and the whole world around them sings. They light up the darkness. We are also vessels of Gods light. Like a clay lantern, we shine God's light. But when we come into the world, we only have an opening at the top, which reflects God's light back up to Him. As we go through rough patches in the world, as we trip in darkness, as we become more and more broken, more of the clay falls away. Cracks begin to run through us. But a beautiful thing happens with these cracks and broken pieces. We don't become *useless*; we become more *useful*. Because through our cracks, God is able to shine his light, and instead of just reflecting his love and light back up to him, we start shining it into the world around us. We shine it through our broken pieces and our cracks. We shine it in God's grace and love that helped us get through our trials. Brokenness doesn't leave us destroyed; it leaves us beautiful. So, don't be ashamed of the hurt, be proud to have been broken, knowing that God can shine the brightest light through you. We were made to be like fireflies and light up the darkness.

Reference Verses

Psalm 34:18
The Lord is close to the brokenhearted; He rescues those whose spirits are crushed.

Psalm 147:3
He heals the brokenhearted and binds up their wounds.

Isaiah 57:15
The high and lofty one who lives in eternity, the Holy One, says this: "I live in the high and holy place with those whose spirits are contrite and humble. I restore the crushed spirit of the humble and revive the courage of those with repentant hearts."

1 Corinthians 15:43-44
Our bodies are buried in brokenness, but they will be raised in glory. They are buried in weakness, but they will be raised in strength. They are buried as natural human bodies, but they will be raised as spiritual bodies. For just as there are natural bodies, there are also spiritual bodies.

2 Corinthians 4:6-7
For God, who said, "Let there be light in the darkness," has made this light shine in our hearts so we could know the glory of God that is seen in the face of Jesus Christ. We now have this light shining in our hearts, but we ourselves are like fragile clay jars containing this great treasure. This makes it clear that our great power is from God, not from ourselves.

2 Corinthians 12:9

Each time he said, "My grace is all you need. My power works best in weakness." So now I am glad to boast about my weaknesses, so that the power of Christ can work through me.

Matthew 5:3-5

God blesses those who are poor and realize their need for him, for the Kingdom of Heaven is theirs. God blesses those who mourn, for they will be comforted. God blesses those who are humble, for they will inherit the whole earth.

Journal Space

Day 4:

Broken Mirrors

My dad used to always tell me that when my mom was pregnant with me, they both pictured a blue-eyed, blonde-haired baby. But it was an image they couldn't believe would be true, because they both had brown hair and dark eyes. So, my dad went as far as to hang up a picture of a brown-haired, brown-eyed baby, so that he would be able to picture me as he thought I would arrive. Surprise, surprise, I was a blue-eyed, toe-headed blonde! My parents always discussed what a wonder it was that they both had brown eyes and I had been born with blue eyes. One day in high school, my mom was repeating the same story to me, only this time I saw things differently. Now that I wasn't a child looking up to my parents, I could see my mom eye-to-eye, and I could see something she couldn't. I said, "Mom, you do realize that you have hazel green eyes, right? They aren't brown." Not only are my mom's eyes hazel, they are actually quite light in color, definitely not brown. She argued with me that her eyes were indeed brown. I walked her to the mirror and made her look into it—really look into it. She fell silent, as years' worth of a false belief fell away. Her jaw dropped, and she said, "Oh my God, I have hazel eyes! How did I never notice this?"

My mom grew up in a very chaotic environment. My grandmother was mentally ill, and the rest of the household ended up walking on eggshells and picking up the pieces of her messes. When chaos fills a home, it makes it hard to see clearly. My mom's eyes were darker than her mother's, so her parents had always told her that she had brown eyes, and she just believed them. Why wouldn't she? They were her parents; they wouldn't lie about her eye color. What would the motive be? The challenge is, when you are dealing with chaos and living in a home that is broken, you can't see things clearly. Unhealed brokenness begets more brokenness. Glass mirrors are not the only things that shine our reflection back to us. The people and things in our lives also act as mirrors. So, what happens when the reflection we see is in a broken mirror? You can't see your true image in a broken mirror.

Not all of the people who are part of our lives are healthy or whole. They don't all have clear vision. Some of them are broken mirrors. Some of them offer a clouded, fragmented reflection. They reflect what they see back to you, but the image you see through their eyes is distorted. They tell you lies about yourself. They reflect an image of you that is not true. When broken people come into our lives briefly, we often see the fault in their assessment of us. But what happens when those people are the voices and the reflections you see and hear day in and day out for years? What happens when those people are our family or partners? When you hear something enough, or see something enough, there is a part of you that can't help but believe the lie. However, whether you believe it or not, a lie does not become the truth.

What lies have you believed about yourself? Stupid, unworthy, too sensitive, too much, not enough, heavy, ugly, unlovable, unworthy, crazy? Are these lies you've been told or believed about yourself? When you look in the mirror, what do you see? What are the voices you hear, that you wish you could quiet?

Know this: we live in a broken world, with broken people. We look in broken mirrors and wonder why we don't like our own reflections. But the mirror God reflects us through is not broken, and it's not dirty. It is shiny and it is clean. He sees the beautiful creation He made you to be. He sees the complex and beautiful gifts that you bring to the world, and He wants you to see yourself through His eyes, in His mirror. He wants you to know that you are beautiful, that you are loved, that you are worthy.

Reference Verses

Genesis 1:27
So God created human beings in his own image. In the image of God he created them; male and female he created them.

Proverbs 6:12-19
What are worthless and wicked people like? They are constant liars, signaling their deceit with a wink of the eye, a nudge of the foot, or the wiggle of fingers. Their perverted hearts plot evil, and they constantly stir up trouble. But they will be destroyed suddenly, broken in an instant beyond all hope of healing. There are six things the Lord hates—no, seven things he detests: haughty eyes, a lying tongue, hands that kill the innocent, a heart that plots evil, feet that race to do wrong, a false witness who pours out lies, a person who sows discord in a family.

Psalms 12:2-8
Neighbors lie to each other, speaking with flattering lips and deceitful hearts. May the Lord cut off their flattering lips and silence their boastful tongues. They say, "We will lie to our heart's content. Our lips are our

own—who can stop us?" The Lord replies, "I have seen violence done to the helpless, and I have heard the groans of the poor. Now I will rise up to rescue them, as they have longed for me to do." The Lord's promises are pure, like silver refined in a furnace, purified seven times over. Therefore, Lord, we know you will protect the oppressed, preserving them forever from this lying generation, even though the wicked strut about, and evil is praised throughout the land.

Psalm 139:13-14

You made all the delicate, inner parts of my body and knit me together in my mother's womb. Thank you for making me so wonderfully complex! Your workmanship is marvelous—how well I know it.

2 Corinthians 6:14 NIV

Do not be yoked together with unbelievers. For what do righteousness and wickedness have in common? Or what fellowship can light have with darkness?

2 Corinthians 11: 13-15

These people are false apostles. They are deceitful workers who disguise themselves as apostles of Christ. But I am not surprised! Even Satan disguises himself as an angel of light. So it is no wonder that his servants also disguise themselves as servants of righteousness. In the end they will get the punishment their wicked deeds deserve.

1 John 4:1

Dear friends, do not believe everyone who claims to speak by the Spirit. You must test them to see if the spirit they have comes from God. For there are many false prophets in the world.

Acts 20:29-30
I know that false teachers, like vicious wolves, will come in among you after I leave, not sparing the flock. Even some men from your own group will rise up and distort the truth in order to draw a following.

Ephesians 4:25
So stop telling lies. Let us tell our neighbors the truth, for we are all parts of the same body.

Journal Space

_____

_____

_____

_____

_____

_____

Day 5:

Unapologetically You

There was one time I found myself seriously perturbed by something someone had said to me. I initially felt the need to explain myself more thoroughly or prove my point so that maybe they might understand with a clean perspective. However, before I sat down to write what I would say, the Holy Spirit whispered, "Why? What do you have to prove to this person?" It stopped me in my tracks as I realized the answer was … nothing. I don't need to prove myself to that man, or anyone else. All I need to do is be the best version of me that I possibly can be. Because, at the end of the day, it's between me and God, and I'm the one who needs to be able to look in the mirror and like what I see. I may not be everyone's cup of tea, but I know that who I am matters to some people; it blesses them, and I'm happy to be me. There are so many amazing people in this world: people with beautiful quirks, amazing stories, and fire inside, some who are shy, and some who live out loud. But there are two things we all have in common: we are all human, and we are all uniquely ourselves.

Humanity makes us imperfect, it makes us quirky, it makes us weird; it means we make mistakes, but it's also beautiful. Humanity allows us to feel, to have compassion, to give, and to receive. There are no two people in this world who are exactly the same, and that in and of itself is so gut-wrenchingly beautiful to me. That means that each of us has something special to contribute to the world. Who we are matters. Our humanity also gives us this one unfortunate flaw, however: insecurity. I know so many incredible people who are afraid that they are not enough.

I wish that I could show everyone who doesn't see their worth, everyone who is afraid to be themselves, how truly precious they are. That is a truth that can't be told; it has to be felt. But I wanted to leave you all with this thought today: you are perfectly imperfect, and the world needs you, just as you are. Embrace yourself, love yourself, and if there's something you aren't proud of that you can change, change it. All we can be is the best version of ourselves. So, I challenge you each day to be shamelessly you. If you are moved to dance, then dance like no one's watching. Don't live this life to prove anything to anyone else. Live this life unabashedly, as you. Do the things that bring you joy and do them unapologetically. God made us unique for a purpose. We are all needed, and we all have value, so embrace your uniqueness even when others don't understand. The world needs you, just as you are.

Reference Verses

Psalm 139:1
O Lord, you have examined my heart and know everything about me.

Psalm 139:13
You made all the delicate, inner parts of my body and knit me together in my mother's womb. Thank you for making me so wonderfully complex! Your workmanship is marvelous—how well I know it.

Jeremiah 1:5

I knew you before I formed you in your mother's womb. Before you were born I set you apart and appointed you as my prophet to the nations."

Luke 12:7

And the very hairs on your head are all numbered. So don't be afraid; you are more valuable to God than a whole flock of sparrows. (See also Matthew 10:30)

1 Corinthians 12:12-26

The human body has many parts, but the many parts make up one whole body. So it is with the body of Christ. Some of us are Jews, some are Gentiles, some are slaves, and some are free. But we have all been baptized into one body by one Spirit, and we all share the same Spirit. Yes, the body has many different parts, not just one part. If the foot says, "I am not a part of the body because I am not a hand," that does not make it any less a part of the body. And if the ear says, "I am not part of the body because I am not an eye," would that make it any less a part of the body? If the whole body were an eye, how would you hear? Or if your whole body were an ear, how would you smell anything? But our bodies have many parts, and God has put each part just where he wants it. How strange a body would be if it had only one part! Yes, there are many parts, but only one body. The eye can never say to the hand, "I don't need you." The head can't say to the feet, "I don't need you." In fact, some parts of the body that seem weakest and least important are actually the most necessary. And the parts we regard as less honorable are those we clothe with the greatest care. So we carefully protect those parts that should not be seen, while the more honorable parts do not require this special care. So God has put the body together such that extra honor and care are given to those parts that have less dignity. This makes for harmony among the members, so that all the members care for each other. If one part suffers, all the parts suffer with it, and if one part is honored, all the parts are glad.

Romans 8:27-37

And the Father who knows all hearts knows what the Spirit is saying, for the Spirit pleads for us believers in harmony with God's own will. And we know that God causes everything to work together for the good of those who love God and are called according to his purpose for them. For God knew his people in advance, and he chose them to become like his Son, so that his Son would be the first born among many brothers and sisters. And having chosen them, he called them to come to him. And having called them, he gave them right standing with himself. And having given them right standing, he gave them his glory. What shall we say about such wonderful things as these? If God is for us, who can ever be against us? Since he did not spare even his own Son but gave him up for us all, won't he also give us everything else? Who dares accuse us whom God has chosen for his own? No one—for God himself has given us right standing with himself. Who then will condemn us? No one— for Christ Jesus died for us and was raised to life for us, and he is sitting in the place of honor at God's right hand, pleading for us. Can anything ever separate us from Christ's love? Does it mean he no longer loves us if we have trouble or calamity, or are persecuted, or hungry, or destitute, or in danger, or threatened with death? As the Scriptures say, "For your sake we are killed every day; we are being slaughtered like sheep." No, despite all these things, overwhelming victory is ours through Christ, who loved us.

Journal Space

_____

_____

_____

_____

_____

_____

Day 6:

Armor of Insecurities

How many insecurities have we built up like a fortress around us? Putting those insecurities and hurts on like armor, to keep people away from our vulnerable places, and, at the same time, preventing ourselves from the love and nurturing that we need and deserve. You are not perfect. I am not perfect. No human being in this entire world is perfect. The very word human means we are not God, and, therefore, we are not perfect. How much has a fear of this very imperfection made you shut others out? Your brokenness is meant to be loved just as much as your strength. God says it is in our weakness that He is made strong (2 Cor. 12:9). We all bleed, we all cry, we all get tired and weary, we all get confused. We all need to be nurtured and loved right where we are. Trust that you don't have to be perfect. Trust that you don't have to be put together; you can come as you are. You can be a weepy, sobbing, hysterical mess and still be loved. You can come broken and bruised and still be treated with tender care. You can come dirty and weary and still be received with open arms and a warm bed. The Bible tells all who are weary to come to Jesus, and they will find rest. His burden is easy, and His yoke is light. (Matthew 11:28-30).

No one wants a perfect person; otherwise, their own imperfections will be judged and shunned. People want real, and even if real is not what they want, it's what they need. We all need to know that we are not alone in our brokenness. We all need to know that we are seen and known and understood. Jesus says that He knew you before you were born. He knit you together in your mother's womb. (Jer. 1:5, Psalm 139:15). God knew what you would walk through. He knew you before you set foot on this earth. He created and loved you for a purpose. He created you to be loved and cherished. He created us to be in communion with each other, no matter how broken we are. God said, "It is not good that man should be alone." (Gen. 2:18 NKJV). He also said, "Love your neighbor as yourself." (Mark 12:31). Think of what a blessing it is to be able to give, how good it feels to be able to give to your loved ones and feel as though you are able to help them. It gives you a sense of purpose to be able to help and give to others. It makes you feel empowered being the giver. Don't deprive the people in your lives of the same gift. Don't deny them of the gift of giving to you as well.

When someone you love hurts, don't you feel the desire to bless them and ease their pain? When someone you know is struggling or needs advice, or just a kind and listening ear, don't you want to be the one they feel safe coming to? I guarantee we all feel this desire to give to and bless those we love. We all desire to feel needed and wanted. When we shut down our own feelings, build up fortresses of insecurity around us, and don't allow anyone to see our brokenness, we deny the people who love us the gift of feeling their worth. We deny them the gift of feeling needed. We deny them the gift of trusting them in our pain to love us through it and not judge us for it. Your vulnerability is a beautiful gift. It's what makes you human, and it's what allows love to come in and work through you. Don't allow the pain of insecurity to keep you from the blessing of love and vulnerability.

Reference Verses

Genesis 2:18
Then the Lord God said, "It is not good for the man to be alone. I will make a helper who is just right for him."

Jeremiah 1:5
"I knew you before I formed you in your mother's womb. Before you were born I set you apart and appointed you as my prophet to the nations."

Psalm 118:6
The Lord is for me, so I will have no fear. What can mere people do to me?

Ephesians 6:10-17
A final word: Be strong in the Lord and in his mighty power. Put on all of God's armor so that you will be able to stand firm against all strategies of the devil. For we are not fighting against flesh-and-blood enemies, but against evil rulers and authorities of the unseen world, against mighty powers in this dark world, and against evil spirits in the heavenly places. Therefore, put on every piece of God's armor so you will be able to resist the enemy in the time of evil. Then after the battle you will still be standing firm. Stand your ground, putting on the belt of truth and the body armor of God's righteousness. For shoes, put on the peace that comes from the Good News so that you will be fully prepared. In addition to all of these, hold up the shield of faith to stop the fiery arrows of the devil. Put on salvation as your helmet, and take the sword of the Spirit, which is the word of God.

2 Corinthians 12:9

Each time he said, "My grace is all you need. My power works best in weakness." So now I am glad to boast about my weaknesses, so that the power of Christ can work through me.

Hebrews 10:22-25

Let us go right into the presence of God with sincere hearts fully trusting him. For our guilty consciences have been sprinkled with Christ's blood to make us clean, and our bodies have been washed with pure water. Let us hold tightly without wavering to the hope we affirm, for God can be trusted to keep his promise. Let us think of ways to motivate one another to acts of love and good works. And let us not neglect our meeting together, as some people do, but encourage one another, especially now that the day of his return is drawing near.

1 John 4:18

Such love has no fear, because perfect love expels all fear. If we are afraid, it is for fear of punishment, and this shows that we have not fully experienced his perfect love.

Mark 12:30-31

'And you must love the Lord your God with all your heart, all your soul, all your mind, and all your strength.' The second is equally important: 'Love your neighbor as yourself.' No other commandment is greater than these.

Matthew 11:28-30

Then Jesus said, "Come to me, all of you who are weary and carry heavy burdens, and I will give you rest. Take my yoke upon you. Let me teach you, because I am humble and gentle at heart, and you will find rest for your souls. For my yoke is easy to bear, and the burden I give you is light."

Philippians 4:6-9

Don't worry about anything; instead, pray about everything. Tell God what you need, and thank him for all he has done. Then you will experience God's peace, which exceeds anything we can understand. His peace will guard your hearts and minds as you live in Christ Jesus. And now, dear brothers and sisters, one final thing. Fix your thoughts on what is true, and honorable, and right, and pure, and lovely, and admirable. Think about things that are excellent and worthy of praise. Keep putting into practice all you learned and received from me—everything you heard from me and saw me doing. Then the God of peace will be with you.

Journal Space

_____

_____

_____

_____

_____

_____

Day 7:

Community

Friendship and community are powerful gifts. When we are cut off from others, it's like living in a box where light and air can't get in, a box where our own thoughts can drive us mad. It's a place where the lies we are told get spoken into the empty space like an echo chamber, ringing in our ears. Sometimes isolation happens because someone in your life has tried to keep you from other people, keep you for themselves, and control your environment. Maybe they do this in the name of love but love never drives disconnection from others. Perhaps they do this so they can be everything to you, and make sure that no one else fills any voids or takes their "place." Regardless of the reasons, control and isolation are not love; they are the opposite. Sometimes isolation is of our own making, driven by shame, embarrassment, hurt, overwhelm, pride. Maybe we feel safe in our boxes, where no one else can reach us, and we don't have to face the light that shines and exposes every truth. One thing is for sure, whether another person has put you in a box of isolation, or whether it's a box of your own making, nothing good comes from living closed off from the rest of the world. We are called into community and relationship with others. We are meant to have rich friendships and share life with many people. We are meant to share our experiences and hear and learn from others' experiences. We are made to live in community.

We've all gone through struggles and trials in life, where we doubted ourselves or wondered what the right thing to do was. Sometimes it's in the moments of uncertainty that we close ourselves off the most, fearing that no one else will understand, or if they knew the truth, they wouldn't stand by us. Or we fear that someone may tell us the wrong thing and lead us astray. But it's moments like these that we need to reach out the most, moments when our mind becomes a mess of confusion and we need some fresh air and fresh perspective to clear out the cobwebs. In moments like this, it's important to know that we are not alone, that someone sees us and cares, that someone has our back, no matter what choices we make or the outcome.

Friends and loved ones are who get us through the darkest times in life. They lend encouragement. They remind us who we are. They lift us up when we are down. They bring light into situations where we cannot see clearly. We often underestimate the power of a smile, a listening ear, a hug, a word of encouragement. We underestimate our impact: how much it means just to be there for someone. Or, we underestimate how much it can help us to just reach out and let someone be there for us.

Each one of us has the power to do small things every day that make a difference, and together, we have the power to do huge things. Alone, we are a drop in the ocean; together, we are a wave crashing into shore, changing the sand forever. When you are hurting and lonely, reach out. When you don't have the answers and don't know what the next step is, lean into those who love you, those who have shown you they care. When you see someone hurting, reach out. When you feel the tug to say something positive to someone, do it. When you have the power to give, give. Together, we can do great things, heal great hurts, and grow closer to God.

Reference Verses

Proverbs 27:17
As iron sharpens iron, so a friend sharpens a friend.

Proverbs 11:30
The seeds of good deeds become a tree of life; a wise person wins friends.

Proverbs 16:28
A troublemaker plants seeds of strife; gossip separates the best of friends.

Proverbs 15:22
Plans go wrong for lack of advice; many advisers bring success.

Proverbs 17:17
A friend is always loyal, and a brother is born to help in time of need.

Proverbs 27:9
The heartfelt counsel of a friend is as sweet as perfume and incense.

Psalm 133:1
How wonderful and pleasant it is when brothers live together in harmony!

Hebrews 10:24-25
Let us think of ways to motivate one another to acts of love and good works. And let us not neglect our meeting together, as some people do, but encourage one another, especially now that the day of his return is drawing near.

Ecclesiastes 4:9-12

Two people are better off than one, for they can help each other succeed. If one person falls, the other can reach out and help. But someone who falls alone is in real trouble. Likewise, two people lying close together can keep each other warm. But how can one be warm alone? A person standing alone can be attacked and defeated, but two can stand back-to-back and conquer. Three are even better, for a triple-braided cord is not easily broken.

Romans 12:4-6, 9-13

Just as our bodies have many parts and each part has a special function, so it is with Christ's body. We are many parts of one body, and we all belong to each other. In his grace, God has given us different gifts for doing certain things well. So if God has given you the ability to prophesy, speak out with as much faith as God has given you ... Don't just pretend to love others. Really love them. Hate what is wrong. Hold tightly to what is good. Love each other with genuine affection, and take delight in honoring each other. Never be lazy, but work hard and serve the Lord enthusiastically. Rejoice in our confident hope. Be patient in trouble, and keep on praying. When God's people are in need, be ready to help them. Always be eager to practice hospitality.

Matthew 18:20

For where two or three gather together as my followers, I am there among them.

1 John 1:7

But if we are living in the light, as God is in the light, then we have fellowship with each other, and the blood of Jesus, his Son, cleanses us from all sin.

Ephesians 4:3-4

Make every effort to keep yourselves united in the Spirit, binding yourselves together with peace. For there is one body and one Spirit, just as you have been called to one glorious hope for the future.

Ephesians 4:15-16

Instead, we will speak the truth in love, growing in every way more and more like Christ, who is the head of his body, the church. He makes the whole body fit together perfectly. As each part does its own special work, it helps the other parts grow, so that the whole body is healthy and growing and full of love.

Ephesians 4:29

Don't use foul or abusive language. Let everything you say be good and helpful, so that your words will be an encouragement to those who hear them.

Romans 1:11-12

For I long to visit you so I can bring you some spiritual gift that will help you grow strong in the Lord. When we get together, I want to encourage you in your faith, but I also want to be encouraged by yours.

Galatians 6:10

Therefore, whenever we have the opportunity, we should do good to everyone—especially to those in the family of faith.

1 Thessalonians 2:8

We loved you so much that we shared with you not only God's Good News but our own lives, too.

Journal Space

_____

_____

_____

_____

_____

_____

Day 8:

Whisper

Does anyone ever come to your mind when you are saying your prayers? Do you ever get a fleeting thought only to have it come to pass within a few hours? Have you ever had a tug on your heart that just tells you to go somewhere, or do something, even when you don't understand why? Have you ever had a silent revelation, or a thought come to you, that brought with it complete peace and grounding? When we think of God speaking, and giving us revelations, we often think of big signs, or a big supernatural voice, or being absolutely overcome in a moment. He is the God of the universe after all, the one who created Heaven and earth, the oceans, and the stars. He is larger than life, but is His voice? Many of the signs we know from the Old Testament were big extravagant signs, like the parting of the seas, or the burning bush. However, in 1 Kings 19:12, the Bible also tells us that when Elijah heard from the Lord, God wasn't in the big earthquake, or the raging wind, or the fire, God was the gentle whisper, the still small voice that came after the raging loud displays. Many of the signs we see in the Bible also happened in a time before the Holy Spirit dwelt within us. Christ told His disciples that when He left, they would get something even better: the Holy Spirit, God in us.

How often do we look for the big signs in the outer world, and not listen to the still small voice within us? Sometimes the voice inside us is just a whisper. A whisper that speaks life, a whisper that supports your dreams, a whisper that brings guidance, peace, and certainty, a whisper that tells you it's time for a change when your heart is just not happy. Sometimes the Holy Spirit speaks to us when we are praying, and it brings people and situations to our minds and gives us guidance for them or asks us to cover them in prayer. Sometimes the Holy Spirit speaks to us through circumstances and the Bible, and it tugs at our hearts and gives us new revelations as we read. Sometimes it speaks to us in the late hours when our minds are quiet, and the voice is clear as day giving us guidance and support. The Holy Spirit is present in everyone who believes in Jesus and loves Him. It is the quiet whisper of your heart that can be easily drowned out by the noise of the world if you are not careful. We have to take time to quiet ourselves and our minds, and slow down the world around us, so we can hear. We have to tune our ears away from the noise of the world, and into the still small voice that lives inside each of us. The Spirit is there, as our counselor, our guide, our friend. And when He speaks, He brings peace, He brings certainty, He brings Joy, and He brings freedom.

Reference Verses

1 Kings 19:11-12

"Go out and stand before me on the mountain," the Lord told him. And as Elijah stood there, the Lord passed by, and a mighty windstorm hit the mountain. It was such a terrible blast that the rocks were torn loose, but the Lord was not in the wind. After the wind there was an earthquake, but the Lord was not in the earthquake. And after the earthquake there was a fire, but the Lord was not in the fire. And after the fire there was the sound of a gentle whisper.

Isaiah 11:2 ESV

And the Spirit of the Lord shall rest upon him, the Spirit of wisdom and understanding, the Spirit of counsel and might, the Spirit of knowledge and the fear of the Lord.

John 14:26-27

But when the Father sends the Advocate as my representative—that is, the Holy Spirit—he will teach you everything and will remind you of everything I have told you. "I am leaving you with a gift—peace of mind and heart. And the peace I give is a gift the world cannot give. So don't be troubled or afraid."

John 16:13-14

When the Spirit of truth comes, he will guide you into all truth. He will not speak on his own but will tell you what he has heard. He will tell you about the future. He will bring me glory by telling you whatever he receives from me.

Acts 1:5

"John baptized with water, but in just a few days you will be baptized with the Holy Spirit."

Acts 2:17-18

"In the last days," God says, "I will pour out my Spirit upon all people. Your sons and daughters will prophesy. Your young men will see visions, and your old men will dream dreams. In those days I will pour out my Spirit even on my servants—men and women alike—and they will prophesy."

Acts 7:51-52

"You stubborn people! You are heathen at heart and deaf to the truth. Must you forever resist the Holy Spirit? That's what your ancestors did, and so do you! Name one prophet your ancestors didn't persecute! They even killed the ones who predicted the coming of the Righteous One— the Messiah whom you betrayed and murdered.

Galatians 5:20-23

idolatry, sorcery, hostility, quarreling, jealousy, outbursts of anger, selfish ambition, dissension, division, envy, drunkenness, wild parties, and other sins like these. Let me tell you again, as I have before, that anyone living that sort of life will not inherit the Kingdom of God. But the Holy Spirit produces this kind of fruit in our lives: love, joy, peace, patience, kindness, goodness, faithfulness, gentleness, and self-control. There is no law against these things!

1 Thessalonians 5:19-22

Do not stifle the Holy Spirit. Do not scoff at prophecies, but test everything that is said. Hold on to what is good. Stay away from every kind of evil.

Romans 8:14-16

For all who are led by the Spirit of God are children of God. So you have not received a spirit that makes you fearful slaves. Instead, you received God's Spirit when he adopted you as his own children. Now we call him, "Abba, Father." For his Spirit joins with our spirit to affirm that we are God's children.

Romans 8:26-28

And the Holy Spirit helps us in our weakness. For example, we don't know what God wants us to pray for. But the Holy Spirit prays for us with groanings that cannot be expressed in words. And the Father who knows all hearts knows what the Spirit is saying, for the Spirit pleads for us believers in harmony with God's own will. And we know that God causes everything to work together for the good of those who love God and are called according to his purpose for them.

Romans 9:1

With Christ as my witness, I speak with utter truthfulness. My conscience and the Holy Spirit confirm it.

Romans 15:13 ESV

May the God of hope fill you with all joy and peace in believing, so that by the power of the Holy Spirit you may abound in hope.

1 Corinthians 12:7-11

A spiritual gift is given to each of us so we can help each other. To one person the Spirit gives the ability to give wise advice; to another the same Spirit gives a message of special knowledge. The same Spirit gives great faith to another, and to someone else the one Spirit gives the gift of healing. He gives one person the power to perform miracles, and another the ability to prophesy. He gives someone else the ability to discern whether a message is from the Spirit of God or from another spirit. Still another person is given the ability to speak in unknown languages, while another is given the ability to interpret what is being said. It is the one and only Spirit who distributes all these gifts. He alone decides which gift each person should have.

2 Corinthians 3:17 NIV

Now the Lord is the Spirit, and where the Spirit of the Lord is, there is freedom.

Journal Space

_____

_____

_____

_____

_____

_____

Day 9:

Walls of Fear

Have you ever felt like no matter what you did, you just kept hitting a wall in your life? Have you ever felt like your dream or healing in a situation was over a barrier that you just couldn't seem to break through? I'm sure we all have things in our lives that seem impossible. I'm sure we all have challenges in life that feel like major barriers. But how many of those barriers are imaginary? How many of those walls exist solely in our minds? God says in Matthew 17:20 that if we have faith, even the size of a mustard seed, we can move mountains. If we can move a mountain with our faith, then, surely, we can tear down a wall.

Many of the walls that exist in our lives are nothing but our fears piled up, brick by brick, and cemented together with the lies we believe about ourselves. Our fears can pile so high that it becomes like a castle wall, making a clear path seem blocked, when, in reality, it's open for us to walk through. "For God has not given us a spirit of fear, but of power, and of love, and of a sound mind." (2 Timothy 1:7 NKJV). We have power through Jesus Christ to tear down walls and move mountains. Sometimes, we have to embrace our power, step out in faith, and just do what terrifies us. We have to consciously remove those bricks of fear and start making holes in the walls we've created. The beauty is that even one brick removed compromises the wall, giving you a view of the other side, and bringing the barrier that much closer to crashing down. Sometimes we just have to make one right decision at a time, take one chance at a time, until we've removed so many bricks of fear from the wall that it comes crumbling down and disappears, and we see clearly for the first time that it was never there at all. If we can't slay the dragons in our minds, we'll never slay the dragons in our physical lives. Let's start removing bricks and bring imaginary walls crashing down. There is freedom beyond fear, freedom beyond the imaginary barriers we create in our minds. Jesus said, "you will know the truth and the truth will set you free" (John 8:32). Let's claim that freedom now, in Jesus' name. It is in Freedom, after all, that God intended us to live our lives.

Reference Verses

Deuteronomy 31:6
So be strong and courageous! Do not be afraid and do not panic before them. For the Lord your God will personally go ahead of you. He will neither fail you nor abandon you."

2 Kings 6:16
"Don't be afraid!" Elisha told him. "For there are more on our side than on theirs!"

Psalm 118:6
The Lord is for me, so I will have no fear. What can mere people do to me?

Galatians 5:1
So Christ has truly set us free. Now make sure that you stay free, and don't get tied up again in slavery to the law.

John 6:20
But he called out to them, "Don't be afraid. I am here!"

John 8:32
And you will know the truth, and the truth will set you free."

1 John 4:18
Such love has no fear, because perfect love expels all fear. If we are afraid, it is for fear of punishment, and this shows that we have not fully experienced his perfect love.

2 Timothy 1:7
For God has not given us a spirit of fear and timidity, but of power, love, and a sound mind.

Philippians 4:6
Don't worry about anything; instead, pray about everything. Tell God what you need, and thank him for all he has done.

Romans 8:31
What shall we say about such wonderful things as these? If God is for us, who can ever be against us?

Matthew 10:30-31
And the very hairs on your head are all numbered. So don't be afraid; you are more valuable to God than a whole flock of sparrows.

Matthew 17:20

"You don't have enough faith," Jesus told them. "I tell you the truth, if you had faith even as small as a mustard seed, you could say to this mountain, 'Move from here to there,' and it would move. Nothing would be impossible."

Mark 5:36

But Jesus overheard them and said to Jairus, "Don't be afraid. Just have faith."

Journal Space

_____

_____

_____

_____

_____

_____

Day 10:

Holding Too Many Things

Breakthroughs rarely happen without a peeling away, a letting go, a shedding of the old, so we can put on the new. As a kid, I remember hearing the story of the little boy with the pickle jar. The little boy wanted a pickle, but when he saw the pickle jar full of pickles, he got excited, and tried to grab multiple pickles at the same time. Once his hand was full of pickles, he tried to pull them out of the jar, but couldn't. His hand was stuck in the jar. He was holding too many things at once, and, as a result, couldn't get what he wanted: a pickle. He had to let the handful of pickles go and only take one in order to get the pickle. Life is like that. We juggle so many things on a daily basis. We have dreams and goals we strive for and try to reach, but it's hard to move quickly—or at all—when we are burdened by the weight of too many things.

We all have things we need to let go of. Maybe they are beliefs that no longer serve us, perhaps they are negative things we've been told about ourselves. Some of us carry the weight of responsibility that isn't ours. We feel the need to help everyone, or we feel like we are responsible for everyone and everything. Maybe we believe that if we let go, if we breathe, if we stop taking responsibility for everything that goes wrong, or everyone that's hurting, or for every project, that everything will come crashing down around us. But maybe, just maybe, it's letting go of those things that will actually propel us into our dreams. They say if you always do what you've always done, you will always get what you always got. I want to run the race and win, not lose because I was bogged down by weight I didn't need to carry. I want to eat that pickle, not get stuck because I couldn't bring myself to let go of the rest. I want to shed everything in me that has ever built a wall between me and my dreams. Let's win this race and enjoy a pickle together at the finish line!

Reference Verses

Numbers 11:14
I can't carry all these people by myself! The load is far too heavy!

Psalm 142:3
When I am overwhelmed, you alone know the way I should turn.

Proverbs 12:25
Worry weighs a person down; an encouraging word cheers a person up.

Hebrews 12:1
Therefore, since we are surrounded by such a huge crowd of witnesses to the life of faith, let us strip off every weight that slows us down, especially the sin that so easily trips us up. And let us run with endurance the race God has set before us.

Luke 12:15
Then he said, "Beware! Guard against every kind of greed. Life is not measured by how much you own."

Matthew 11:28
Then Jesus said, "Come to me, all of you who are weary and carry heavy burdens, and I will give you rest."

Philippians 4:6-7
Don't worry about anything; instead, pray about everything. Tell God what you need, and thank him for all he has done. Then you will experience God's peace, which exceeds anything we can understand. His peace will guard your hearts and minds as you live in Christ Jesus.

Matthew 23:4
They crush people with unbearable religious demands and never lift a finger to ease the burden.

Journal Space

_____

_____

_____

_____

_____

_____

Day 11:

Balance

We live in a broken and unbalanced world, a world of extremes with little alignment. But God is a God of balance; He grounds us. He knows that you can't have forgiveness without justice or the world would be a dark place. He also knows that a world without grace is devoid of hope. Everything in this world has its place: anger, joy, tears, laughter, justice, and grace. The problem arises when we give too much weight to one thing. We live in a society where people are either totally self-centered, self-righteous, and entitled or they sacrifice themselves, give everything they have to others, and have nothing left. Neither of these extremes is good or right, but it can be so hard to find the balance.

I've met so many Christians who believe that in order to live a Godly life they have to deny themselves, but this couldn't be further from the truth. God made you just as you are for a reason. To live healthy, fulfilled lives that shine God's light, we need to invest in ourselves, not deny ourselves. Many of us spend so much time and money invested in other people and other endeavors that we forget to take time to invest in ourselves and our own personal well-being. When we invest in ourselves, and our joys, we inadvertently give to the world and those around us. Because when we are happy, that is when we shine the brightest. We can't give to others if we don't first fill ourselves.

We should be striving to find ourselves, to accept ourselves, to grow ourselves, to see who God made us to be, to peel away all the layers of habits we have added to our lives that are not truly us. We should be taught to accept ourselves more, love ourselves more, encourage ourselves more, embrace our ideas and feelings more, allow ourselves to choose happiness, and follow our heart's desires. This doesn't mean you follow every whim that brings temporary relief. This means that you exercise wisdom. You look at the consequences and ask if what you are doing is really leading to what you truly want, or if it's hindering you. God created the desires in our hearts and it says in His word that when we love the Lord and delight in Him, he gives us the desires of our hearts; He doesn't deny them.

There is a sick fixation in some churches on self-sacrifice. But what a sad world it would be if everyone constantly denied themselves and lived in misery. Doesn't happiness shine far more light than sadness and sacrifice? There is also a fixation on guilt in some churches, and a belief that if we are all sinners, we are bad at the core. But to believe that denies so much truth in the bible. The Bible clearly says that God created us in His image (Gen. 1:27). If God is good, and God is love, and we are created in His image, then we are innately good. Are we human? Yes. Do we mess up? Yes. But who we are still matters, and there is goodness in us.

It says in the bible that God knit us together in our mother's womb, and that we were fearfully and wonderfully made (Psalm 139:13-14). This means that God made us to be uniquely us. We serve a purpose in the world. Our desires matter and have a purpose, our happiness matters, who we are and what we do matters. We have a purpose. In fact, it could be said that all sin comes, not from embracing ourselves, but from forgetting who we are. If we lose sight of our own value and uniqueness, we make choices that don't serve our purpose. If we forget our worth, we accept treatment that is unacceptable and get caught in a cycle of unhealthy behavior. When we forget how much our individuality matters, we often end up trying to fit into a box of other people's beliefs and wants, instead of following our own gut.

We were all given a conscience and an intuition. We were all given unique gifts and desires to grace this world with. Please don't take the gift that you are for granted. Don't deny yourself. Seek yourself. Listen to the whispers of your heart. Feel your desires, your aches, your laughter. Seek God and ask Him to show you how loved you are. Smell, Taste, hear, feel, experience, explore, and learn more about yourself. Pay attention to feelings that arise in different situations. Recognize discomfort when things don't feel right, and delight when you are doing something you love. Allow your love to lead you.

God gave us His Holy Spirit to guide us. The spirit in us is our intuition, the voice that makes us hesitate when something just doesn't feel right, the voice that says no when we are violated, the voice that says yes, take the risk when we are scared. It's the voice that whispers: you are loved, you are enough, you matter. When we believe in God, and love God, His Spirit lives in us and His desires echo in our hearts. So, don't deny the tickle in your gut. Don't deny your passions and your love. Live freely, knowing that when you shine, you shine the light of God into the world. You shine the brightest when you are happy, and it is your light that leads people to truth, to God.

Reference Verses

Genesis 1:27
So God created human beings in his own image. In the image of God he created them; male and female he created them.

Psalm 37:4
Take delight in the Lord, and he will give you your hearts desires.

Proverbs 24:24-25
A judge who says to the wicked, "you are innocent," will be cursed by many people and denounced by the nations. But it will go well for those who convict the guilty; rich blessings will be showered on them.

Isaiah 30:18 NIV
Yet the Lord longs to be gracious to you; therefore he will rise up to show you compassion. For the Lord is a God of justice. Blessed are all who wait for him!

Psalm 139:13-16
You made all the delicate, inner parts of my body and knit me together in my mother's womb. Thank you for making me so wonderfully complex! Your workmanship is marvelous—how well I know it. You watched me as I was being formed in utter seclusion, as I was woven together in the dark of the womb. You saw me before I was born. Every day of my life was recorded in your book. Every moment was laid out before a single day had passed.

Ephesians 4:16
He makes the whole body fit together perfectly. As each part does its own special work, it helps the other parts grow, so that the whole body is healthy and growing and full of love.

Romans 12:6-8
In his grace, God has given us different gifts for doing certain things well. So if God has given you the ability to prophesy, speak out with as much faith as God has given you. If your gift is serving others, serve

them well. If you are a teacher, teach well. If your gift is to encourage others, be encouraging. If it is giving, give generously. If God has given you leadership ability, take the responsibility seriously. And if you have a gift for showing kindness to others, do it gladly.

1 Peter 4:10

God has given each of you a gift from his great variety of spiritual gifts. Use them well to serve one another.

1 Cor. 12:4-27

There are different kinds of spiritual gifts, but the same Spirit is the source of them all. There are different kinds of service, but we serve the same Lord. God works in different ways, but it is the same God who does the work in all of us. A spiritual gift is given to each of us so we can help each other. To one person the Spirit gives the ability to give wise advice; to another the same Spirit gives a message of special knowledge. The same Spirit gives great faith to another, and to someone else the one Spirit gives the gift of healing. He gives one person the power to perform miracles, and another the ability to prophesy. He gives someone else the ability to discern whether a message is from the Spirit of God or from another spirit. Still another person is given the ability to speak in unknown languages, while another is given the ability to interpret what is being said. It is the one and only Spirit who distributes all these gifts. He alone decides which gift each person should have. The human body has many parts, but the many parts make up one whole body. So it is with the body of Christ. Some of us are Jews, some are Gentiles, some are slaves, and some are free. But we have all been baptized into one body by one Spirit, and we all share the same Spirit. Yes, the body has many different parts, not just one part. If the foot says, "I am not a part of the body because I am not a hand," that does not make it any less a part of the body. And if the ear says, "I am not part of the body because

I am not an eye," would that make it any less a part of the body? If the whole body were an eye, how would you hear? Or if your whole body were an ear, how would you smell anything? But our bodies have many parts, and God has put each part just where he wants it. How strange a body would be if it had only one part! Yes, there are many parts, but only one body. The eye can never say to the hand, "I don't need you." The head can't say to the feet, "I don't need you." In fact, some parts of the body that seem weakest and least important are actually the most necessary. And the parts we regard as less honorable are those we clothe with the greatest care. So we carefully protect those parts that should not be seen, while the more honorable parts do not require this special care. So God has put the body together such that extra honor and care are given to those parts that have less dignity. This makes for harmony among the members, so that all the members care for each other. If one part suffers, all the parts suffer with it, and if one part is honored, all the parts are glad. All of you together are Christ's body, and each of you is a part of it.

Journal Space

_____

_____

_____

_____

_____

_____

Day 12:

Righteous Rage

Have you ever felt the flame of anger rising up in your chest? Burning there, like an energy that needs to escape? I'm not talking about anger that lashes out or loses its temper. I don't mean anger over a disappointment or a perceived slight. I'm talking about the anger that slowly burns and grows, as the gasoline of love and injustice fuels its flames. The kind of anger that is fueled by disgust over the good things of God being twisted and perverted. This is not a hot temper. This is a righteous rage that energizes you to preparation and action. It gives you a deep desire to make things right and restore what's lost in whatever capacity you can. How many of us grow up in the church, or just in life, believing that anger is bad—that anger is destructive, and causes sin? While there is a compulsive and arrogant rage that is not healthy, there is also a very righteous and Godly rage.

There are many times that God gets angry with His people in Scripture. Even Jesus gets angry with people and calls them out and rebukes them. The difference is that God's anger comes from obvious injustice and sin against Him. He gets angry when His people are being persecuted and mistreated. He gets angry at abuse and greed, and He gets angry when people raise things above Him in idolatry. 1 Corinthians 5:11 says we are not to associate with anyone who calls himself a Christian who is sexually immoral, or greedy, or an idolater, or verbally abusive, or a drunkard, or a swindler. Do not even eat with such a person. God gets angry when something He meant for good gets twisted into something used for harm, and He expects our anger against these things as well. Scripture goes as far as saying we are to remove these evil people from among us in (1 Cor. 5:13). In Ephesians 4:26 (NHEB), we are actually commanded to "Be angry, but do not sin."

So, what does it mean to be angry and not sin? What is the difference between Godly, righteous anger and sinful anger? We have it ingrained in us, by society and most churches, to believe that anger is a bad, evil, and unhealthy emotion, but the truth is that anger is both healthy and Godly when it is anger in its purest form—anger about injustice and sin. Anger gets distorted often by sinful hearts into bitterness, which destroys the holder, and revenge, which causes damage and chaos unless it is reserved for the Lord. But those things are not pure anger; they are what happen to anger when we don't use it for Godly purposes or give it over to God. Godly anger is not about insisting on your own way and getting offended when you don't get what you want. It isn't the frustration you feel when someone runs late, doesn't call back right away, or doesn't do what you hope they will. Godly anger is anger at sin—true sin. Sin against people, that either harms the innocent, or keeps the offender and innocent trapped in slavery. Sin is the perversion of things that God made to be good, twisting them into evil. It takes what is meant to be Holy and distorts it into something painful, wrong, and entrapping. It takes things like marriage, which was meant to be Holy and good, and distorts it through abuse, perverting what God intended for good with sin. We should be horrified and enraged by these things. You see, Godly anger is driven and fed by love—not ego, pure love. It is the anger you experience when a child is attacked and the pain for them rises up in your chest and causes you to get protective. Righteous anger is fueled by love, and a desire to see broken people healed and whole. Righteous anger is a desire to see the persecuted and harmed healed and receiving justice. And it's a desire to see the lost turn from their sin and become Saved. With true Godly anger, there is both love and sadness at the need for punishment.

God desires for everyone to be Saved, and we are called to be "slow to anger." God is patient with us, so we are to be patient with each other, not lashing out, but confronting sin. Anger has a purpose in its pure form. Anger's purpose is to drive us into action to stop sin. So, how do we do this? It says in Matthew 18:15-17 that when someone has sinned against us, we are to go to them in private, rebuke them of the sin, and give them a chance to repent. If they do not turn from their ways, we are to get others in the community involved to help them see the error of their ways and their sin and try to save them. However, if even this does not work, we are to cut them out of the community. 1 Cor. 5:13 specifically states that we are to "remove the evil" people from among us. We are not to put up with evil and sin, but to get angry at it, take action, and remove it from our midst. Anger can show us when there is unrighteousness and we are in need of a change. It energizes us to take the steps needed to make healthy changes in our own lives by removing toxic people and making changes in the world, by standing up for those who do not or cannot stand up for themselves. It also teaches that if we struggle to stop sin on our own, in private, it is time to get the community involved to support you in stopping the sin or removing the evil from your community. We are called to be angry! And to not sin.

So, the next time you feel angry, ask yourself: where is this anger coming from? Is it anger bred from my ego, as a perceived slight? Or is this anger coming from love and a desire for healing, restoration, and goodness? If your anger comes from love and protectiveness, it is a righteous rage, and it deserves to be acknowledged and then have action taken. I do not mean go out and seek revenge; vengeance is the Lord's alone (Rom. 12:19-21). However, take action to remove the evil from among you, rebuke it, and try to bring reconciliation. Don't be afraid to get others in the community involved to help if you are unable to put a stop to it yourself. And finally, remove it from your midst if real remorse and change does not occur. We all have feelings for a reason; they are God given, to inform us of what our soul is crying out for. Embrace your anger as an agent of healthy change and seek God to follow through.

Reference Verses

2 Kings 17:18
Because the Lord was very angry with Israel, he swept them away from his presence. Only the tribe of Judah remained in the land.

Proverbs 6:16-20
There are six things the Lord hates—no, seven things he detests: haughty eyes, a lying tongue, hands that kill the innocent, a heart that plots evil, feet that race to do wrong, a false witness who pours out lies, a person who sows discord in a family.

1 Corinthians 5:2-7
You are so proud of yourselves, but you should be mourning in sorrow and shame. And you should remove this man from your fellowship. Even though I am not with you in person, I am with you in the Spirit. And as though I were there, I have already passed judgment on this man in the name of the Lord Jesus. You must call a meeting of the church. I will be present with you in spirit, and so will the power of our Lord Jesus. Then you must throw this man out and hand him over to Satan so that his sinful nature will be destroyed and he himself will be saved on the day the Lord returns. Your boasting about this is terrible. Don't you

realize that this sin is like a little yeast that spreads through the whole batch of dough? Get rid of the old "yeast" by removing this wicked person from among you. Then you will be like a fresh batch of dough made without yeast, which is what you really are. Christ, our Passover Lamb, has been sacrificed for us.

1 Corinthians 5:11

I meant that you are not to associate with anyone who claims to be a believer yet indulges in sexual sin, or is greedy, or worships idols, or is abusive, or is a drunkard, or cheats people. Don't even eat with such people.

1 Corinthians 5:13

God will judge those on the outside; but as the Scriptures say, "You must remove the evil person from among you."

2 Corinthians 6:14-18

Don't team up with those who are unbelievers. How can righteousness be a partner with wickedness? How can light live with darkness? What harmony can there be between Christ and the devil? How can a believer be a partner with an unbeliever? And what union can there be between God's temple and idols? For we are the temple of the living God. As God said, "I will live in them and walk among them. I will be their God, and they will be my people. Therefore, come out from among unbelievers, and separate yourselves from them, says the Lord. Don't touch their filthy things, and I will welcome you. And I will be your Father, and you will be my sons and daughters, says the Lord Almighty."

Ephesians 4:26 ESV

Be angry and do not sin; do not let the sun go down on your anger,

Ephesians 5:5-14 NIV

For of this you can be sure: No immoral, impure or greedy person—such a person is an idolater—has any inheritance in the kingdom of Christ and of God. Let no one deceive you with empty words, for because of such things God's wrath comes on those who are disobedient. Therefore do not be partners with them. For you were once darkness, but now you are light in the Lord. Live as children of light (for the fruit of the light consists in all goodness, righteousness and truth) and find out what pleases the Lord. Have nothing to do with the fruitless deeds of darkness, but rather expose them. It is shameful even to mention what the disobedient do in secret. But everything exposed by the light becomes visible—and everything that is illuminated becomes a light. This is why it is said: "Wake up, sleeper, rise from the dead, and Christ will shine on you."

Matthew 18:15-17

"If another believer sins against you, go privately and point out the offense. If the other person listens and confesses it, you have won that person back. But if you are unsuccessful, take one or two others with you and go back again, so that everything you say may be confirmed by two or three witnesses. If the person still refuses to listen, take your case to the church. Then if he or she won't accept the church's decision, treat that person as a pagan or a corrupt tax collector."

Romans 1:18

But God shows his anger from heaven against all sinful, wicked people who suppress the truth by their wickedness.

Romans 2:7-10

He will give eternal life to those who keep on doing good, seeking after the glory and honor and immortality that God offers. But he will pour out his anger and wrath on those who live for themselves, who refuse to obey the truth and instead live lives of wickedness. There will be trouble and calamity for everyone who keeps on doing what is evil—for the Jew first and also for the Gentile. But there will be glory and honor and peace from God for all who do good—for the Jew first and also for the Gentile.

Romans 12:19-21

Dear friends, never take revenge. Leave that to the righteous anger of God. For the Scriptures say, "I will take revenge; I will pay them back," says the Lord. Instead, "If your enemies are hungry, feed them. If they are thirsty, give them something to drink. In doing this, you will heap burning coals of shame on their heads." Don't let evil conquer you, but conquer evil by doing good.

2 Timothy 2:23-26

Again I say, don't get involved in foolish, ignorant arguments that only start fights. A servant of the Lord must not quarrel but must be kind to everyone, be able to teach, and be patient with difficult people. Gently instruct those who oppose the truth. Perhaps God will change those people's hearts, and they will learn the truth. Then they will come to their senses and escape from the devil's trap. For they have been held captive by him to do whatever he wants.

Journal Space

_____

_____

_____

_____

_____

_____

Day 13:

Change

Change. A scary topic in some ways, and yet it unfolds in the world all around us. Change is a part of our everyday lives. It is reflected in our seasons, our sunrises, and our sunsets. Change must happen for us to live, breathe, and grow, and yet, for so many of us, just thinking about change is terrifying. Why? Because change is scary. Change is hard. It's the unknown, the breaking of habits deeply ingrained in us, the grieving of something that was to make room for something that will be. Change is the letting go, the moving on, and the fighting harder. Change is painful. Change is grief. It's the loss of one thing to make way for something different. And yet, change is necessary and beautiful. It's what makes us grow. It's what makes way for us to fulfill our dreams and receive the blessings God has in store for us. It's the setting free of our spirits and the breaking of our chains.

There are times when we can see the good and the blessings in the changes in our lives, but that doesn't always mean that those transitions are easy. We may be leaving a really bad situation, breaking bad habits, and coming into good things, but, ironically, when we deal with a change, we still deal with the grief of saying goodbye. It's like parts of us are dying off that needed to fall away.

There are major transitional periods in life we all face, just like the changing of the seasons. Moving to new places, becoming a parent, transitioning from school into the work world, ending unhealthy relationships—our lives are rife with changes. But, it's not just outer changes; the truth is that the outer changes are a reflection of our inner changes. When we set out on new adventures, they are exciting, but excitement can also make way for tears. Tears of letting go, saying goodbye, and moving forward. Change, no matter how good, is terrifying and painful. It is a process, just like a rose bud, so tightly bound, that finally blooms. There are growing pains. I don't know about you, but I want to be the flower that opens its petals and blooms in its full beauty. I know the process is arduous. I know it means holding on and letting go at the same time, but I'm along for the ride, and I will ride through the laughter of excitement and the tears of fear and letting go, because I want to see the end result. How about you?

Reference Verses

Ecclesiastes 3:1-8
For everything there is a season, a time for every activity under heaven. A time to be born and a time to die. A time to plant and a time to harvest. A time to kill and a time to heal. A time to tear down and a time to build up. A time to cry and a time to laugh. A time to grieve and a time to dance. A time to scatter stones and a time to gather stones. A time to embrace and a time to turn away. A time to search and a time to quit searching. A time to keep and a time to throw away. A time to tear and a time to mend. A time to be quiet and a time to speak. A time to love and a time to hate. A time for war and a time for peace.

Isaiah 43:19

For I am about to do something new. See, I have already begun! Do you not see it? I will make a pathway through the wilderness. I will create rivers in the dry wasteland.

Ezekiel 36:26 NIV

I will give you a new heart and put a new spirit in you; I will remove from you your heart of stone and give you a heart of flesh.

Hebrews 13:8

Jesus Christ is the same yesterday, today, and forever.

James 1:17

Whatever is good and perfect is a gift coming down to us from God our Father, who created all the lights in the heavens. He never changes or casts a shifting shadow.

Joshua 1:9

This is my command—be strong and courageous! Do not be afraid or discouraged. For the Lord your God is with you wherever you go.

1 Corinthians 6:11

Some of you were once like that. But you were cleansed; you were made holy; you were made right with God by calling on the name of the Lord Jesus Christ and by the Spirit of our God.

1 Corinthians 15:51-52

But let me reveal to you a wonderful secret. We will not all die, but we will all be transformed! It will happen in a moment, in the blink of an eye, when the last trumpet is blown. For when the trumpet sounds, those who have died will be raised to live forever. And we who are living will also be transformed.

2 Corinthians 3:18
So all of us who have had that veil removed can see and reflect the glory of the Lord. And the Lord—who is the Spirit—makes us more and more like him as we are changed into his glorious image.

2 Corinthians 5:17
This means that anyone who belongs to Christ has become a new person. The old life is gone; a new life has begun!

Philippians. 4:6-8
Don't worry about anything; instead, pray about everything. Tell God what you need, and thank him for all he has done. Then you will experience God's peace, which exceeds anything we can understand. His peace will guard your hearts and minds as you live in Christ Jesus. And now, dear brothers and sisters, one final thing. Fix your thoughts on what is true, and honorable, and right, and pure, and lovely, and admirable. Think about things that are excellent and worthy of praise.

Ephesians 4:22-24 NIV
You were taught, with regard to your former way of life, to put off your old self, which is being corrupted by its deceitful desires; to be made new in the attitude of your minds; and to put on the new self, created to be like God in true righteousness and holiness.

Titus 3:5 NIV
He saved us, not because of righteous things we had done, but because of his mercy. He saved us through the washing of rebirth and renewal by the Holy Spirit

Journal Space

_____

_____

_____

_____

_____

_____

Day 14:

Moving Through the Unknown

There are times in life when the path that we are on feels more like a labyrinth. Every twist and turn is uncharted territory. We can see the steps directly in front of us, but we can't see what is around the next corner. We don't know if the path we are on leads to a dead end or freedom. Where nothing around us is familiar, and every day is a new experience. In moments like these, it can seem like we are feeling our way through the dark and are delighted when we can successfully take the next step without falling. Each day is living in the unknown and a realm of possibility, because when everything is new and you don't know the outcome, anything is possible. This is both terrifying, and absolutely freeing, all rolled into one! It's not that anything is wrong. In fact, life may seem to be moving into great directions, and yet, sometimes even the good things in life can be scary. When you've had trauma in your past, good times can feel like you are just waiting for the next shoe to drop or the next trial to hit. When things are good and you care, suddenly, you have something to lose and this can feel overwhelming when you can't see the whole picture. We just have to trust: trust that if we keep walking in faith we won't stumble, trust that God will give us enough light for the next step, trust that there is good in store for us and not disaster, and if we just make the choice to be all in on the journey, and keep feeling our way to the next right step, that everything will somehow work out.

We don't know what exactly the path holds, and we don't know the outcome yet. We move forward in the in-between and step with hope. We can't see the end of the story, but maybe that's okay. Maybe it's not about the end of the story, but the chapter that we're on—this trail, this moment, this day. We have to remind ourselves daily to be okay with the process, to stop and look around and enjoy the view, because it is not easy for us to be in this unfamiliar place. Even though you may be able to see all of the amazing possibilities that lay ahead, being in this place is scary, emotional, and vulnerable. Vulnerability means being unguarded; it means you can be hurt, but it also means you can be loved and love in return. And, it means that you can be seen, really seen, and understood—a terrifyingly beautiful thing. It is something to embrace, to relish, to juice the experience for all it's worth, pain, fear, tears, laughter and all. The unknown isn't so scary if we lean into God and trust that he will give us just enough light for the next step.

Reference Verses

Job 12:22
He uncovers mysteries hidden in darkness; he brings light to the deepest gloom.

Jeremiah 29:11
"For I know the plans I have for you," says the Lord. "They are plans for good and not for disaster, to give you a future and a hope."

Jude 1:24

Now all glory to God, who is able to keep you from falling away and will bring you with great joy into his glorious presence without a single fault.

Joshua 1:9

This is my command—be strong and courageous! Do not be afraid or discouraged. For the Lord your God is with you wherever you go.

Psalm 116:8 NASB

For You have rescued my soul from death, my eyes from tears, my feet from stumbling.

Psalm 121:3 NASB

He will not allow your foot to slip; He who keeps you will not slumber.

Psalm 140:4 NIV

Keep me safe, LORD, from the hands of the wicked; protect me from the violent, who devise ways to trip my feet.

Psalm 145:14 NASB

The LORD sustains all who fall and raises up all who are bowed down.

Proverbs 4:12

When you walk, you won't be held back; when you run, you won't stumble.

Proverbs 3:6

Seek his will in all you do, and he will show you which path to take.

1 Corinthians 13:11-13

When I was a child, I spoke and thought and reasoned as a child. But when I grew up, I put away childish things. Now we see things imperfectly, like puzzling reflections in a mirror, but then we will see everything with perfect clarity. All that I know now is partial and incomplete, but then I will know everything completely, just as God now knows me completely. Three things will last forever—faith, hope, and love—and the greatest of these is love.

John 12:46

I have come as a light to shine in this dark world, so that all who put their trust in me will no longer remain in the dark.

Journal Space

_____

_____

_____

_____

_____

_____

Day 15:

Forgiveness

Forgiveness: a powerful word with a powerful meaning when it is used right. However, the words love and forgiveness get tossed around like simple greetings in our society and lose their true meaning. Popular psychology, and even many churches, push you to forgive your offenders, claiming that it is the answer to healing, to God's blessings, and so much more, but that's where the teaching stops. Forgiveness in modern culture is treated like candy in a vending machine that can and should be handed out easily and freely. But what does God say and teach about forgiveness? Does God say we should forgive if the offender continues the offense? Does God teach that we are to be candy vendors, doling out chocolate bars of forgiveness with no true repentance? Does God say we should forget an offense, act as though it never happened, and give no consequences for poor choices or actions? The way the word forgiveness is thrown around, you would think that these things are what God calls us to, but that couldn't be farther from the truth. God is a God of justice, truth, love, and grace. It's easy to focus on the feel-good, positive message of God's grace. God's grace is a huge part of His character, as God is a God of love. However, when we take the grace out of context and we make grace more important than justice and truth, than grace is no longer a loving action.

God is love. We know this to be true from the Bible; our God is the definition of love. We also learn in the Bible that God is a God of justice and truth, who doesn't rejoice in what's wrong, but rejoices in what's right. God hates evil—even evil people. God gets angry with unrepentant hearts. God loved us so much that when we were yet sinners, He gave His only son to die for our sins, so that we could live and live life abundantly. And yet, there is another piece to that message. While the work was already done in Christ and we don't have to strive for grace, we do have to repent of our sins and accept Christ into our hearts. You see, God's forgiveness is free, absolutely free. We don't have to pay for God's grace and forgiveness. We don't have to strive for it, and it doesn't matter how far or long we've been off of God's path, He still offers forgiveness. However, His forgiveness does require two small things: repentance and love. So, if God won't forgive an unrepentant heart that continues to harm others with no remorse, how could we expect to forgive them? God tells us in Luke 17:3-4 (NIV) that "If your brother or sister sins against you, rebuke them; and if they repent, forgive them." This is an instruction to forgive, but that instruction comes in three parts: 1) Rebuke them, 2) Let them repent, 3) *If* they repent, forgive them. God doesn't say that you should forgive them if they don't repent. He says forgive them *if* they repent. God speaks of forgiveness again in 1 John 1:9 (NIV). He says, "If we confess our sins, he is faithful and just and will forgive us our sins and purify us from all unrighteousness." Here again God says *if*. "If we confess our sins" God is faithful to forgive us. You see, where love may be unconditional, forgiveness is not. Forgiveness is always available, no matter how far someone has fallen, but it doesn't come without repentance. God desires to forgive everyone. Many times, in the Bible, he even offers people his warnings to repent and prevent destruction. In every case of true repentance, they are forgiven and not destroyed.

Another phrase people like to toss around about forgiveness is, "forgive and forget," but does forgiveness mean that you forget what was done and act as if nothing ever happened? No. God forgives, but he still allows the consequences of our actions to unfold. God forgives, but He doesn't forget, and He doesn't want His people to forget either. Throughout the Bible, we see stories illustrating people sinning and coming back to God, but when they return, God doesn't forget the offense. He expects changed behavior; He expects us to make right what has been wrong. This even happens with the disciples. Before Jesus died on the cross, He told Peter that Peter would deny Him three times, and Peter swore he wouldn't. (Matthew 26:34-35) Peter fell short on his promise to Jesus and did in fact sin against Him and deny Him three times. However, when Jesus returned, He gave Peter the opportunity to not only repent, but to make right what had been done. God didn't forget the offense. In John 21:15-17 Jesus asks Peter three times if he loves Him. Jesus asks him three times because that is the number of times that Peter denied Jesus. The offense wasn't forgotten, but God gave Peter the opportunity to make it right and show changed behavior. When we forgive people, that doesn't mean that we should forget their offense and trust them. It also doesn't mean that we should go back to them if the offense was caused in the context of a relationship. We can forgive someone without allowing them back in our lives or our circle of trust on the same level that they once were. The bible tells us to be aware and wise. In Proverbs 14:15-16 and Proverbs 22:3 it says that we are to be shrewd, look out for danger, and protect ourselves. It says we should not believe every word spoken but ponder each step. So, forgive, let go of bitterness and resentment and rage, but be cautious and guard your heart. This doesn't mean we make anyone prove to us that they are trustworthy by putting them through tests or monitoring them closely.

That is toxic for both parties. It does, however, mean that we are to be cautious and discerning.

When we speak of forgiveness, most of the time forgiveness is "other"-centered, but there is another very important piece to forgiveness. Sometimes the very person we need to forgive is not someone on the outside, but ourselves. How quick are we to forgive others of small offenses, but how deeply do we hold on to our own mistakes and beat ourselves up for them? There are times when we are our own worst enemies. There are times when our own minds hold us captive in un-forgiveness for mistakes that we have made or things we think we failed at. We need to practice forgiveness of our own hearts and minds. Recognize what happened, or what you feel you did wrong, and maybe talk to another person that you feel safe with and can trust. Sometimes we hold things against ourselves that aren't true offenses; they are just the enemy twisting God's word and our fears to attack us. This is why talking to a safe person can be very helpful. At times, the very thing you need to apologize to yourself for is simply being too hard on yourself or taking responsibility for things that weren't your fault. Once you have recognized the offense, apologize to yourself and to God. Let that apology sink in, and then choose to do differently. Doing differently is a daily walk. It is a reminder to quiet the voice of criticism in your own head when it pops up. It is a reminder to take deep breaths and look to God and pray when you get upset, instead of reacting or jumping to conclusions. It is the day-to-day choices and every step of the walk. Take it easy on yourself and know that you are worth just as much forgiveness, care, and love as anyone else in your life. And please know that it doesn't matter what you have done, God knows your heart, and He loves you. He sees the pain you've gone through and he knows that you desire change. He is faithful and just to forgive. And you, dear, are His treasure.

Reference Verses

Isaiah 5:20
What sorrow for those who say that evil is good and good is evil, that dark is light and light is dark, that bitter is sweet and sweet is bitter.

Isaiah 26:10
Your kindness to the wicked does not make them do good. Although others do right, the wicked keep doing wrong and take no notice of the Lord's majesty.

Psalm 37:8
Stop being angry! Turn from your rage! Do not lose your temper—it only leads to harm.

Psalm 103:12 NKJV
As far as the east is from the west, so far has he removed our transgressions from us.

Proverbs 14:15
Only simpletons believe everything they're told! The prudent carefully consider their steps.

Proverbs 22:3
A prudent person foresees danger and takes precautions. The simpleton goes blindly on and suffers the consequences.

Proverbs 28:13
People who conceal their sins will not prosper, but if they confess and turn from them, they will receive mercy.

Proverbs 25:19

Putting confidence in an unreliable person in times of trouble is like chewing with a broken tooth or walking on a lame foot.

Luke 17:3-4 NIV

So watch yourselves. "If your brother or sister sins against you, rebuke them; and if they repent, forgive them."

Ephesians 4:31 NIV

Get rid of all bitterness, rage and anger, brawling and slander, along with every form of malice.

1 John 1:9 NIV

If we confess our sins, he is faithful and just and will forgive us our sins and purify us from all unrighteousness.

John 21:15-17

After breakfast Jesus asked Simon Peter, "Simon son of John, do you love me more than these?" "Yes, Lord," Peter replied, "you know I love you." "Then feed my lambs," Jesus told him. Jesus repeated the question: "Simon son of John, do you love me?" "Yes, Lord," Peter said, "you know I love you." "Then take care of my sheep," Jesus said. A third time he asked him, "Simon son of John, do you love me?" Peter was hurt that Jesus asked the question a third time. He said, "Lord, you know everything. You know that I love you." Jesus said, "Then feed my sheep.

Acts 3:19 NIV

Repent, then, and turn to God, so that your sins may be wiped out, that times of refreshing may come from the Lord.

Acts 26:20

I preached first to those in Damascus, then in Jerusalem and throughout all Judea, and also to the Gentiles, that all must repent of their sins and turn to God—and prove they have changed by the good things they do.

Colossians 1:13-14 NIV

For he has rescued us from the dominion of darkness and brought us into the kingdom of the Son he loves, in whom we have redemption, the forgiveness of sins.

Hebrews 10:26 NASB

For if we go on sinning willfully after receiving the knowledge of the truth, there no longer remains a sacrifice for sins

Galatians 5:7-10

You were running the race so well. Who has held you back from following the truth? It certainly isn't God, for he is the one who called you to freedom. This false teaching is like a little yeast that spreads through the whole batch of dough! I am trusting the Lord to keep you from believing false teachings. God will judge that person, whoever he is, who has been confusing you.

1 Corinthians 5:9-13

When I wrote to you before, I told you not to associate with people who indulge in sexual sin. But I wasn't talking about unbelievers who indulge in sexual sin, or are greedy, or cheat people, or worship idols. You would have to leave this world to avoid people like that. I meant that you are not to associate with anyone who claims to be a believer yet indulges in sexual sin, or is greedy, or worships idols, or is abusive, or is a drunkard, or cheats people. Don't even eat with such people. It isn't my responsibility to judge outsiders, but it certainly is your responsibility to judge those inside the church who are sinning. God will judge those on the outside; but as the Scriptures say, "You must remove the evil person from among you."

1 Corinthians 13:4-5

Love is patient and kind. Love is not jealous or boastful or proud or rude. It does not demand its own way. It is not irritable, and it keeps no record of being wronged.

Matthew 18:15-18

"If another believer sins against you, go privately and point out the offense. If the other person listens and confesses it, you have won that person back. But if you are unsuccessful, take one or two others with you and go back again, so that everything you say may be confirmed by two or three witnesses. If the person still refuses to listen, take your case to the church. Then if he or she won't accept the church's decision, treat that person as a pagan or a corrupt tax collector. "I tell you the truth, whatever you forbid on earth will be forbidden in heaven, and whatever you permit on earth will be permitted in heaven."

Matthew 26:34-35

Jesus replied, "I tell you the truth, Peter—this very night, before the rooster crows, you will deny three times that you even know me." "No!" Peter persisted. "Even if I have to die with you, I will never deny you!" And all the other disciples vowed the same.

Journal Space

_____

_____

_____

_____

_____

_____

Day 16:

You Matter

You matter. There is so much in this life that leads us to question ourselves and what the right thing to do is. In certain circumstances, we wonder what we should do, how we should respond, or how we should act. We can be left unsure of what is okay to give in to or give up. How much sacrifice is okay and how much is too much. Is sacrifice really ok at all? Jesus died so that we could live. He died to set the captives free, and yet, it is so easy to put ourselves back into sacrifice and slavery.

I'm not saying that we shouldn't give of ourselves. We should absolutely give of ourselves, of our time, of our love, of our energy. Giving is exactly what Christ called us to—sharing the good message and giving of ourselves. But sacrifice and giving are two very different things. We are to love our neighbors as ourselves. (Mark 12:31). So, how can we give of ourselves when we sacrifice who we are? How can we give of ourselves when our boundaries are crossed, our desires and needs are left unmet, and we are running on empty? You matter. Who you are matters. You matter in your full, unfiltered, weird, quiet, loud, goofy glory. You matter to others, you matter to this world, and you matter to

God. Your opinions matter, your beliefs matter, your thoughts matter, your feelings matter, and your boundaries matter. Who you are matters. Who you are is needed. You matter to the people who care about you.

There are people in this world who need you. They don't need a watered-down version of you. They don't need a contained version of you. They need you exactly as you are, with all of your opinions and feelings and thoughts, all of your boundaries, all of your quirks. You have a purpose. God made you and your heart and your thoughts and feelings as they are for a reason, because you are needed, and you are loved. *You* matter.

There is nothing on this earth—no belief, no dream, no duty, no responsibility, no person, nothing—that is worth compromising who you are: your needs, your feelings, your wants, and your boundaries. The moment we begin to give ourselves away to other people's want of us, without being true to our own desires and needs, is the moment we tell ourselves the lie that we don't matter. It's the moment we put another person's want of us above God. It's the moment we hurt the people close to us, because they need us, and they need us flourishing. It's the moment that we stop being truly effective. We stop shining the light we are meant to shine, and we stop being able to give of ourselves in a real way. You matter. God made you exactly as you are for a reason. God knit you together in your mother's womb. (Psalm 139:13). You deserve to be happy, and the people who love and need you deserve to see you healthy and prosperous. **You matter**.

Reference Verses

Psalm 139:13-19 NIV

For you created my inmost being; you knit me together in my mother's womb. I praise you because I am fearfully and wonderfully made; your works are wonderful, I know that full well. My frame was not hidden from you when I was made in the secret place, when I was woven together in the depths of the earth. Your eyes saw my unformed body; all the days ordained for me were written in your book before one of them came to be.

Jeremiah 1:5 NIV
"Before I formed you in the womb I knew you, before you were born I set you apart; I appointed you as a prophet to the nations."

Isaiah 49:15-16
Can a mother forget the baby at her breast and have no compassion on the child she has borne? Though she may forget, I will not forget you! See, I have engraved you on the palms of my hands; your walls are ever before me.

Ephesians 2:10 NIV
For we are God's handiwork, created in Christ Jesus to do good works, which God prepared in advance for us to do.

John 10:10 NIV
The thief comes only to steal and kill and destroy; I have come that they may have life, and have it to the full.

Galatians 5:1 NIV
It is for freedom that Christ has set us free. Stand firm, then, and do not let yourselves be burdened again by a yoke of slavery.

Mark 12:30-31 NIV
"Love the Lord your God with all your heart and with all your soul and with all your mind and with all your strength." The second is this:

"Love your neighbor as yourself." There is no commandment greater than these."

1 Cor. 12:14-26 NIV

Even so the body is not made up of one part but of many. Now if the foot should say, "Because I am not a hand, I do not belong to the body," it would not for that reason stop being part of the body. And if the ear should say, "Because I am not an eye, I do not belong to the body," it would not for that reason stop being part of the body. If the whole body were an eye, where would the sense of hearing be? If the whole body were an ear, where would the sense of smell be? But in fact God has placed the parts in the body, every one of them, just as he wanted them to be. If they were all one part, where would the body be? As it is, there are many parts, but one body. The eye cannot say to the hand, "I don't need you!" And the head cannot say to the feet, "I don't need you!" On the contrary, those parts of the body that seem to be weaker are indispensable, and the parts that we think are less honorable we treat with special honor. And the parts that are unpresentable are treated with special modesty, while our presentable parts need no special treatment. But God has put the body together, giving greater honor to the parts that lacked it, so that there should be no division in the body, but that its parts should have equal concern for each other. If one part suffers, every part suffers with it; if one part is honored, every part rejoices with it.

Matthew 10:29-31

What is the price of two sparrows—one copper coin? But not a single sparrow can fall to the ground without your Father knowing it. And the very hairs on your head are all numbered. So don't be afraid; you are more valuable to God than a whole flock of sparrows.

Isaiah 26:10
Your kindness to the wicked does not make them do good. Although others do right, the wicked keep doing wrong and take no notice of the Lord's majesty.

Matthew 23:4
They crush people with unbearable religious demands and never lift a finger to ease the burden.

Journal Space

Day 17:

Discerning the Voice of God from the Enemy

God speaks. He speaks to our hearts. He speaks through our spirit. He speaks through signs, through visions, through our intuition. He speaks through Scripture. He speaks through others in our lives. He speaks. We have all heard God at points in our lives, urging us in certain directions, speaking to our gut through a deep knowing feeling. God finds ways to speak to all of us through the Holy Spirit. But Scripture also tells us that God is not the only spirit that comes upon us; we have an enemy as well. The devil is also a spirit, and we are in a battle. Scripture tells us we do not fight against flesh and blood, but against principalities and powers of darkness in the spiritual realm. (Eph. 6:12). There is a battle for our spirits, a battle for our minds, and a battle for our souls. The enemy speaks to us as well, and the enemy is a liar. Scripture tells us that the enemy comes to kill, steal, and destroy, but Jesus came to give us life, and life abundant. (John 10:10). Scripture also tells us that the enemy comes dressed as an angel of light. (2 Cor. 11:14). The enemy loves to disguise himself as God, or an angel of God, but where God speaks truth and life, the enemy speaks lies. This tells us that we need to be discerning. We need to be able to sift through the noise, to sift through the voices we hear, and the spirits that come upon us, and discern if what we are feeling and hearing is the voice of God or the voice of the enemy.

From early childhood, God made me a feeling and hearing being. He tuned me in to Him and the people around me. I could feel, and see, and hear more than most. But that also meant that I was in tune with both positive and negative people and things. This caused a lot of anxiety for me. God often told me when those I cared for were in danger, but if God gave warning messages, that also meant the enemy could step in and strike fear in my heart. So, I needed to grow in discernment and seek truth. I sought the truth in two places:

1. In people who had come before me. Those who were happy, healthy, full of the Spirit, and close to God.

2. In the Scripture. When reading Scripture, I quickly learned the importance of context. The Bible isn't one verse or one chapter; it's a whole book. There are many parts to the story, and if we take just one chapter of that book and read it out of context, we don't get the whole story. The enemy loves to use this against us. As we read (2 Cor 11:14), the enemy comes dressed as an angel of light. One of the devil's favorite tools is to take God's word and twist it, to use it against us. The Devil knows if he attacks us outright, it will be too obvious, so instead, he tries to turn us against ourselves through guilt and shame and a twisted perception of God's word.

The number one sign that the devil is speaking or manipulating you is this: the devil brings guilt, shame, and condemnation. The first question to ask yourself when trying to discern a voice is: "does this voice make me feel guilt or shame? Or, does it bring hope and peace?"

God does not make us feel guilty. God does not shame us. God never tells us that we are not enough, or that we have lost everything. God does not condemn us. This is not to say that we never sin, or that God doesn't tell us when we are sinning, but when God speaks to us, it is not to condemn. It is to convict. God's voice will convict you, but He will do it in love. With Godly conviction comes certainty, peace, and hope. God doesn't tell us we've messed up and make us feel bad about all the ways we could have done better. God gives us the roadmap to healing. God knows that we have pain and darkness in our lives that we need to be freed from, and He knows how those things hurt us. When He convicts us, He desires to set us free from harm, and doubt, and fear. God's conviction always brings freedom and peace. Whereas the enemy tries to find ways to make us feel guilty and keep us trapped in darkness, God desires to break our chains. The more the enemy can keep us stuck in a cycle of self-doubt, fear, and uncertainty, the less we can hear the voice of God, and the happier the enemy is. Where God makes all things new, the enemy loves leading us down old paths out of fear, shame, and guilt.

Another favorite tool that the enemy uses against us is fear. The enemy loves to strike fear in our hearts and use that fear to manipulate us. Which brings us to the next question to ask yourself when seeking to discern whether it's God's voice or another voice: "Does this voice come from a place of fear or a place of love?" The enemy loves to remind us of the past hurts in our lives. The enemy loves to tell us that we are not enough, or we are too much, and we will fail. But God's voice comes from a place of love, not fear, and when God guides us, there is no fear. It says in 1 John 4:18 (NKJV) that "There is no fear in love; but perfect love casts out fear, because fear involves torment." When a voice speaks instructions that instill fear and doubt in you, that voice is not from God. This bears clarification, because God's voice does not always lead us to places within our comfort zones. In fact, He often leads us outside of our comfort zones, and outside of what we perceive as normal. You see, throughout our lives, we all develop habits and coping mechanisms that act as survival instincts, but God knows that often our very freedom is outside of these constructs we've made out of self-protection. But, despite how different it may seem, when you hear this voice, it will feel good. It will bring comfort, hope, and clarity, and often it will give you a vision or sense of what good can come from it. It will not leave you in hesitation, wondering if it was God when it calls you into foreign territory; it will come with crystal clear certainty. The enemy will step in and try to tell you all the reasons you are not capable of doing what God has called you to do. The enemy's voice will try to make you too afraid to move forward, but you will still know with certainty that what you heard was true. Fear of the Lord brings excitement and hope, while fear from the enemy brings anxiety and obsessive thinking and tells you that you're not good enough, that you will be rejected, that you are too much. God's word blatantly tells us that we are made in His image, we are loved and accepted, not rejected, and we "can do all things through Christ who strengthens" us. (Phil. 4:13 NKJV). God gives us the deep desires in our hearts; the enemy tries to make us settle for less by telling us we can't have what we truly want and desire. When you find that a voice is shutting down your deepest desires through fear, it is not from God. God calls us to move forward in love. God's guidance causes us to know our power and our worth and to know that we are loved. "God has not given us a spirit of fear, but of power, and of love, and of a sound mind. (2 Tim. 1:7 NKJV).

The final question to ask yourself when you are trying to discern whether a voice is from God may be the most important question of them all: "Is this wise?" God gives us knowledge and wisdom when we seek them from Him. God also allows us to go through experiences in life to teach us. God never leads His people into harm. God never leads you into harmful relationships, situations, or habits. God never leads us into abuse. God may show us a truth that hurts temporarily in order to set us free from a lie, but God never leads us to places and people that harm us. God never leads us into a pit of fire. If we are thrown into the pit of fire, He can rescue us, but He will never lead us there. Only the devil will lead us back to people who harm us, demean us, and undermine us. The devil tells us that we have to strive or prove ourselves. The devil tells us we aren't enough, we didn't do enough. But God tells us that His grace is sufficient. We don't have to strive and try; we just have to walk with Him in love. This doesn't mean you aren't supposed to show up in your life and do good work. It also doesn't mean that the place you are called to will be in your comfort zone. But it does mean you will not be called to prove yourself or strive, and you will not be called back into harm. You can walk an unknown road with wisdom, knowledge, preparation, and the armor of God and be safe. On the contrary, you can walk a very familiar road, that is full of old negative patterns, and be harmed. God unveils truth for us, and once we see the truth, we are to walk in it. When God shows us clear danger, evil, and harm, we are to get away from it, not walk right back into it. God will not lead you into something that will crush your spirit. He leads us into peace, hope, and freedom. We can claim this life of freedom, peace, and abundance as we learn to hear and recognize His voice—the voice of truth—above all others.

Reference Verses

Isaiah 11:2 ESV

And the Spirit of the Lord shall rest upon him, the Spirit of wisdom and understanding, the Spirit of counsel and might, the Spirit of knowledge and the fear of the Lord.

Galatians 5:20-23

Idolatry, sorcery, hostility, quarreling, jealousy, outbursts of anger, selfish ambition, dissension, division, envy, drunkenness, wild parties, and other sins like these. Let me tell you again, as I have before, that anyone living that sort of life will not inherit the Kingdom of God. But the Holy Spirit produces this kind of fruit in our lives: love, joy, peace, patience, kindness, goodness, faithfulness, gentleness, and self-control. There is no law against these things!

Ephesians 6:11-12

Put on all of God's armor so that you will be able to stand firm against all strategies of the devil. For we are not fighting against flesh-and-blood enemies, but against evil rulers and authorities of the unseen world, against mighty powers in this dark world, and against evil spirits in the heavenly places.

John 10:9-10

Yes, I am the gate. Those who come in through me will be saved. They will come and go freely and will find good pastures. The thief's purpose is to steal and kill and destroy. My purpose is to give them a rich and satisfying life.

1 John 4:18

Such love has no fear, because perfect love expels all fear. If we are afraid, it is for fear of punishment, and this shows that we have not fully experienced his perfect love.

2 Corinthians 3:17 NIV

Now the Lord is the Spirit, and where the Spirit of the Lord is, there is freedom.

2 Corinthians 11:13-15

These people are false apostles. They are deceitful workers who disguise themselves as apostles of Christ. But I am not surprised! Even Satan disguises himself as an angel of light. So it is no wonder that his servants also disguise themselves as servants of righteousness. In the end they will get the punishment their wicked deeds deserve.

1 Peter 5:8 ESV

Be sober-minded; be watchful. Your adversary the devil prowls around like a roaring lion, seeking someone to devour.

Philippians 4:7 NIV

And the peace of God, which transcends all understanding, will guard your hearts and your minds in Christ Jesus.

Philippians 4:13

For I can do everything through Christ, who gives me strength.

Romans 15:13 ESV

May the God of hope fill you with all joy and peace in believing, so that by the power of the Holy Spirit you may abound in hope.

2 Timothy 1:7

For God has not given us a spirit of fear and timidity, but of power, love, and self-discipline.

1 Thessalonians 5:19-22

Do not stifle the Holy Spirit. Do not scoff at prophecies, but test everything that is said. Hold on to what is good. Stay away from every kind of evil.

Journal Space

_____

_____

_____

_____

_____

_____

Day 18:

Empty Cups

Have you ever met someone who just shines? It's almost like they put off a light. They are so full of God's love that they radiate. Their presence brightens a room. Their laugh is like music lightening up the entire space, and somehow, you feel safe with them and warm. They shine God's light.

When I was young, I thought I was one of these people. My yearbook was littered with signatures from people telling me how much they loved that I smiled all the time and that my smile always brightened their day. I was the girl who always smiled. The one who was there for everyone else. I was a giver, and I loved being there for friends. I would take on other people's hurt as if it was my own and still wrap them in a warm hug, with a smile on my face. I never complained. I never leaned on them. I never cried or asked for help. I was the happy one. right? Well, I thought so, until one day, it all came crashing down. I was betrayed by a friend, and I realized that I was tired. I had given all I had to everyone else and had nothing left for myself. But I also had nothing left to give anyone else. I became somewhat of a temporary recluse, aside from my daily school activities. I shut down socially. I hid in a cave of my thoughts, fears, and emotions, and I got help to sort them out. I had always believed that I was one of those people who just radiated God's love, but there was one major difference. The people who truly shine God's light are full of the Spirit of God. The key here is that they are full. They radiate His light, and it pours out of them because they are so full that their cup runs over. They have an exceeding abundance of God's love pouring out of them. While I loved God and had His spirit, I had been giving, not in His strength, but my own. I had been giving from my own reserve, not from God's, and as a result, I was totally empty. I needed to learn how to ask and receive. I couldn't help anyone or give to anyone from an empty cup. I had to learn to fill my own cup first.

As Christians, it's easy to take on the role of giver. We give to children, we give to friends, we give to family, we give to work colleagues. We tithe and give to the church. We give of our time to help the community, and often, there are people in our lives who are struggling, and we feel the need to give an extra amount of effort and care to them. Sometimes we give so much that we take on new roles and wear too many hats. We take on the extra roles of caregiver, counselor, forgiver, and rescuer. With most Christian teaching being so focused on giving, we can forget that some of these roles are not hats that we are supposed to wear or loads that we are meant to carry. We often give, and give, and give, until there is nothing left and we are depleted. What are we left with then to share? We have an empty cup. How can we provide water to the thirsty if there is no water in our own cup? How can we even carry the water to the thirsty if we fall down in exhaustion because we ourselves have become dehydrated?

It's so easy to feel like taking time for yourself or doing something for yourself is a selfish act, but it is actually the least selfish thing that you can do. The Bible clearly shows us that self-care is actually a very important part of being close to God and giving to others. You can't give joyfully and lovingly out of an overflow of abundance if you never stop to fill your own cup or take care of your own needs. You can't get water out of parched and dry land. Sometimes the best way to give to other people is to show them by example to take care of themselves. Perhaps we need to live in such a way that we show people that we are important and cherished, and in turn, teach them to treat themselves with the same value. It says in Daniel 10:19 that we are "Precious to God." Shouldn't we be living in such a way that shows that we believe this and honor God? This is what Jesus did. The Word that is often preached in churches is about giving to others and forgiving others, but a key part is left out in this teaching. We are to first allow ourselves to receive and be forgiven. It says in God's Word, "We love, because He first loved us." (1 John 4:19 NIV). He had to fill us with that love before we had the love to pour out on Him and others. It also says in His Word, that we are to love our neighbors as ourselves. (Mark 12:30-31). It is very easy to focus on the first part of this verse "love your neighbors" and lose the ending, which is the most important part: "as yourselves." The verse, as written, assumes and implies that we will automatically protect our own interests, safety, and health, and that we will love ourselves. We are, after all, God's precious children. We are His creation. Our bodies are the temples of the Lord most High, and we are meant to care for ourselves. It says in Ephesians 5:29 (ESV) that "no one ever hated his own flesh, but nourishes and cherishes it." If we do not love ourselves, how can we possibly love others? If we do not love ourselves, but constantly give to others, we put ourselves in a yoke of slavery. When we are enslaved, our captors whip us, wear us out, take from us without giving, use us, and deplete us. This is not how God intended our giving to be. It says in Galatians 5:1 (NIV) that "It is for freedom that Christ has set us free," and we are to stand firm and not let ourselves "be burdened again by a yoke of slavery." It also says in 2 Corinthians 9:7, that God loves cheerful givers. We weren't intended to be captives, but joyful givers.

We were meant to be so full of love and life, and so full of God, that we joyfully give from the abundance of our spirits.

Throughout Scripture, Jesus leads by example, showing us all the balance that we are supposed to find in loving ourselves and giving to others. Jesus knew He had limits in a human body, and He knew that He must be filled with the Spirit of His Father if He was going to be able to give to others. So, Jesus took the time He needed to refresh, revive, and refill. Jesus did this without guilt and without apology. He knew that taking care of Himself and refilling His cup was necessary to do His Father's work. Jesus set boundaries; He took time alone for Himself to refresh, and He didn't accept abuse. Jesus rarely talked about these things. Instead, He shows us through His example what we are expected to do.

We so often say that actions speak louder than words, but somehow, when it comes to the Word of the Lord, we look to the words, instead of looking at the actions in the Word. Jesus sought time alone with God to refresh and renew no matter what anyone was demanding of Him, and he took this time for Himself to refresh unapologetically. Jesus took care to remove himself from danger and abusive people (Luke 4:28-30). He didn't allow people to manipulate Him and pull Him away from His calling or the good He was doing, no matter who they were. He didn't allow people to use their relationships with Him as a sense of entitlement to move Him (Matthew 12:46-50). Jesus allowed Himself to rest and encouraged His disciples to do the same (Mark 6:31-32). He also withdrew on His own, to pray and get filled by God (Luke 5:15-16), and He never apologized for doing this (Luke 2:49). Jesus asked for help and sought comfort from friends when He needed it (Matt. 26:36-38). Jesus showed us time and time again how important it is to take care of your own needs and wants and fill your own cup. He came so that we may "have life and have it to the full." (John 10:10 NIV). So give yourself permission to rest, to set boundaries, to do some good things for yourself. Give yourself permission to take time alone and pray, and ask God to fill you, so that you can be full of light. Do this fearlessly, with no guilt. Give to yourself unapologetically, and "May the God of hope fill you with all joy and peace as you trust in Him, so that you may overflow with hope by the power of the Holy Spirit." (Romans 15:13 NIV).

- Do you ever struggle with guilt around taking time for yourself? If the answer is yes, go to God in prayer and ask Him for his help.
- When in the past have you given until you were depleted?
- What are three ways you can refill your own cup this week?

Reference Verses

Genesis 2:2-3
On the seventh day God had finished his work of creation, so he rested from all his work. And God blessed the seventh day and declared it holy, because it was the day when he rested from all his work of creation.

Daniel 10:19
"Don't be afraid," he said, "for you are very precious to God. Peace! Be encouraged! Be strong!"

2 Corinthians 9:7
You must each decide in your heart how much to give. And don't give reluctantly or in response to pressure. "For God loves a person who gives cheerfully."

Ephesians 5:29 ESV
For no one ever hated his own flesh, but nourishes and cherishes it, just as Christ does the church,

Galatians 5:1

So Christ has truly set us free. Now make sure that you stay free, and don't get tied up again in slavery to the law.

John 10:9-10

Yes, I am the gate. Those who come in through me will be saved. They will come and go freely and will find good pastures. The thief's purpose is to steal and kill and destroy. My purpose is to give them a rich and satisfying life.

1 John 4:18-19

Such love has no fear, because perfect love expels all fear. If we are afraid, it is for fear of punishment, and this shows that we have not fully experienced his perfect love. We love each other because he loved us first.

Luke 2:48-49

His parents didn't know what to think. "Son," his mother said to him, "why have you done this to us? Your father and I have been frantic, searching for you everywhere." "But why did you need to search?" he asked. "Didn't you know that I must be in my Father's house?"

Luke 4:28-30

When they heard this, the people in the synagogue were furious. Jumping up, they mobbed him and forced him to the edge of the hill on which the town was built. They intended to push him over the cliff, but he passed right through the crowd and went on his way.

Luke 5:15-16

But despite Jesus' instructions, the report of his power spread even faster, and vast crowds came to hear him preach and to be healed of their diseases. But Jesus often withdrew to the wilderness for prayer.

Mark 3:7-9

Jesus went out to the lake with his disciples, and a large crowd followed him. They came from all over Galilee, Judea, Jerusalem, Idumea, from east of the Jordan River, and even from as far north as Tyre and Sidon. The news about his miracles had spread far and wide, and vast numbers of people came to see him. Jesus instructed his disciples to have a boat ready so the crowd would not crush him.

Mark 6:31-32

Then Jesus said, "Let's go off by ourselves to a quiet place and rest awhile." He said this because there were so many people coming and going that Jesus and his apostles didn't even have time to eat. So they left by boat for a quiet place, where they could be alone.

Mark 12:30-31

"And you must love the Lord your God with all your heart, all your soul, all your mind, and all your strength." The second is equally important: "Love your neighbor as yourself." No other commandment is greater than these.

Matthew 11:28-30

Then Jesus said, "Come to me, all of you who are weary and carry heavy burdens, and I will give you rest. Take my yoke upon you. Let me teach you, because I am humble and gentle at heart, and you will find rest for your souls. For my yoke is easy to bear, and the burden I give you is light."

Matthew 12:46-50

As Jesus was speaking to the crowd, his mother and brothers stood outside, asking to speak to him. Someone told Jesus, "Your mother and your brothers are standing outside, and they want to speak to you." Jesus asked, "Who is my mother? Who are my brothers?" Then he pointed to his disciples and said, "Look, these are my mother and brothers. Anyone who does the will of my Father in heaven is my brother and sister and mother!"

Matthew 26:36-38

Then Jesus went with them to the olive grove called Gethsemane, and he said, "Sit here while I go over there to pray." He took Peter and Zebedee's two sons, James and John, and he became anguished and distressed. He told them, "My soul is crushed with grief to the point of death. Stay here and keep watch with me."

Romans 15:13-14

I pray that God, the source of hope, will fill you completely with joy and peace because you trust in him. Then you will overflow with confident hope through the power of the Holy Spirit. I am fully convinced, my dear brothers and sisters, that you are full of goodness. You know these things so well you can teach each other all about them.

Journal Space

_____

_____

_____

_____

_____

_____

Day 19:

Imaginary Cages

Have you ever seen a bird in a cage that has the door open, but it still won't fly away? It's gotten so used to captivity that it can't see the open door, and even if it sees the open door, it's gotten so used to the constructs of the cage that it's stopped looking for a way out. When the bird was first caged, it fought being put into the cage, and once the door was shut, it tried to find a way out. It couldn't settle; it hated the confines of the metal. It wanted to be free again, to fly. But the longer it stayed in the cage, the more it lost its will to escape, and the more used to the bars it got. Until one day, the cage felt normal, comfortable even. The memories of flying were so distant it could barely remember the way the breeze felt in its face. At some point, its captor opened the cage door, and the bird didn't even try to fly away. It's gotten so used to the tight space that it doesn't see any other way; even with the open door, it sees no other way of living. I have been that bird. Sitting in the cage of an abusive relationship, with the door wide open, and yet I saw no way out. I met him when I was young, and even though I almost felt suffocated in the beginning by his extreme affection and attention and my gut told me something was off, I told myself that he just liked me and this was what a serious relationship looked like. I told myself it was okay, it was healthy; I just wasn't used to really being wanted so it felt foreign. I told myself to just lean into it and enjoy being wanted so much. But the love bombing of extreme affection slowly dissolved into little digs at my self-esteem and mind games just to keep me on edge. It was subtle, and it was over time. It was confusing. Just when I would get to a point where I thought I couldn't take it anymore, he'd flip the script and start acting nice again. He'd shower me with affection again, just like he had in the beginning, and I'd find myself believing that it was okay, it was better, and I was perfectly content in the cage that he'd placed my life in. But I wasn't. I had to tone down who I was to fit in his cage. I had to constantly push down my own wants, needs, and desires for his. I had to push down my frustrations and anger, because he refused to have conversations that brought any resolution. Somehow, he always ended up calling me crazy, or tearing down my emotions if I ever spoke up. So, I learned not to. My inner voice got used to being mute. I was numb, but I told myself I was happy. But it wasn't true, and I certainly wasn't free. Abuse isn't the only cage in this world. So often in our lives, we are that bird, fit into a tight cage that we once hated, once fought against, but at some point, the cage became so familiar that we forgot there was another way to live.

The cages that we live in are imaginary. They are cages with wide open doors. When Christ died on the cross for us, He died to set us free. He set us free from the law that couldn't save us. He died to set us free from our sin. He died to set us free from the confines and constructs of this world. He broke our chains. He opened our cage doors. He set us free! It says in Gal. 5:1 (NIV), "It is for freedom that Christ has set us free. Stand firm, then, and do not let yourselves be burdened again by a yoke of slavery." And yet so often, we do go right back to slavery and we don't see our own freedom. We don't recognize the gift that we have already been given. Maybe we feel shame for past mistakes, feeling like

they can't be forgiven. Maybe we feel that we've gone too far, or been enslaved too long, and it's too late to get out. Or maybe, we are just so used to the cage that we are afraid to venture beyond it, unsure that there's good beyond the cage, forgetting what a beautiful life we have in freedom. So often we allow ourselves to stay stuck in the yoke of slavery. Walking beyond the cages that we have learned to call home may be terrifying, but it is so worth it. We weren't made to live in tight spaces. We weren't created to live a life controlled by other people or bound up in shame, guilt, and obligation. We were made with a free will; we were made in God's image. We were made free.

When Christ went to the cross, He took all of our bondage and chains, all of our sin, and He crucified it there with his body. In that moment, those chains were all broken and sin was dead. It is done. There is nothing that you can do to win freedom and to earn grace. It was done. In that moment, it was won. We spend so much of our lives trying to be worthy of the cross with this idea that we too are supposed to crucify ourselves, and yet Christ Himself said it is done (John 19:30). You see, the story doesn't end with Christ on the cross; if Christ died there that day, He wouldn't be God, and we wouldn't worship Him. What makes Him Christ is that He rose. He rose so that we would have freedom and eternal life, and that is what we are called to in Him. Christ died so that we could live, and live life abundantly. (John 10:10) Christ died for freedom, and He gives us freedom for freedom's sake. We don't have to earn our freedom; we just have to accept it. We have to accept the love that has set us free and be willing to leave the cages we have been trapped in. The world outside might look large and scary after being stuck in such a tight space, but it's vast and beautiful and full of blessings and joy, and love, and discovery.

What are the cages you have been confined to in your own life? Are they cages that other people have put you in through negative words or control? Are they cages that were created in your own mind out of

fear and obligation, insecurity, and guilt? Whatever they are, know that Christ has already set you free. It's time to claim your freedom. God made us to live in a world of beauty, and freedom, and love. It's time to look out and see that the cages you've been living in are imaginary. It's time to venture out in faith and freedom, into the beautiful world that God gave us.

Reference Verses

Psalm 91:1-11

Those who live in the shelter of the Most High will find rest in the shadow of the Almighty. This I declare about the Lord: He alone is my refuge, my place of safety; he is my God, and I trust him. For he will rescue you from every trap and protect you from deadly disease. He will cover you with his feathers. He will shelter you with his wings. His faithful promises are your armor and protection. Do not be afraid of the terrors of the night, nor the arrow that flies in the day. Do not dread the disease that stalks in darkness, nor the disaster that strikes at midday. Though a thousand fall at your side, though ten thousand are dying around you, these evils will not touch you. Just open your eyes, and see how the wicked are punished. If you make the Lord your refuge, if you make the Most High your shelter, no evil will conquer you; no plague will come near your home. For he will order his angels to protect you wherever you go.

Psalm 107:13-16

"Lord, help!" they cried in their trouble, and he saved them from their distress. He led them from the darkness and deepest gloom; he snapped their chains. Let them praise the Lord for his great love and for the wonderful things he has done for them. For he broke down their prison gates of bronze; he cut apart their bars of iron.

Galatians 5:1

So Christ has truly set us free. Now make sure that you stay free, and don't get tied up again in slavery to the law.

John 8:32

And you will know the truth, and the truth will set you free."

John 8:36

So if the Son sets you free, you are truly free.

John 10:9-10

Yes, I am the gate. Those who come in through me will be saved. They will come and go freely and will find good pastures. The thief's purpose is to steal and kill and destroy. My purpose is to give them a rich and satisfying life.

John 19:30

When Jesus had tasted it, he said, "It is finished!" Then he bowed his head and gave up his spirit.

Luke 10:19 ESV

Behold, I have given you authority to tread on serpents and scorpions, and over all the power of the enemy, and nothing shall hurt you.

Mark 11:23 NIV

"Truly I tell you, if anyone says to this mountain, 'Go, throw yourself into the sea,' and does not doubt in their heart but believes that what they say will happen, it will be done for them."

Romans 8:1-4 ESV

There is therefore now no condemnation for those who are in Christ Jesus. For the law of the Spirit of life has set you free in Christ Jesus from the law of sin and death. For God has done what the law, weakened by the flesh, could not do. By sending his own Son in the likeness of sinful flesh and for sin, he condemned sin in the flesh, in order that the righteous requirement of the law might be fulfilled in us, who walk not according to the flesh but according to the Spirit.

Journal Space

_____

_____

_____

_____

_____

_____

Day 20:

On Paper

When I was a little girl, I learned not to cry. I learned not to admit weakness, and I learned to never ask for help. I grew up with two older brothers, who I loved dearly, but they were much bigger than me, much older, and they loved beating me up. The games they played with me would range from hanging me over the stairwell and threatening to drop me to suffocating me in blankets to normal boy stuff, like spitting on me. I thought this was normal. All siblings fight, right? But when I screamed for help or cried, I wasn't met with comfort, help, or apology. I was screamed at. I was told to shut up, that my parents were trying to work. I was told to be quiet, so they could safely drive, because my complaining was making driving dangerous and they couldn't do anything about my brothers' behavior while we were on the road. If I cried because I was sad or hurting, I was accused of throwing a tantrum—I was not heard, and I was not held. The only time we really cried together was when someone died. So, I learned that death was the only reason to feel real feelings. The other times I felt sad or angry or needed help? I just had to tough it out. I had to put on a smile. I had to pretend it didn't hurt and bury my feelings, because, God forbid, if I got caught crying, I would be made to feel badly for feeling at all, or even worse I'd be yelled at for having an emotional reaction other than exuberance. I started believing that my truth, and my vulnerability, was too much for people, so I shut it down. I lived with a plastered-on smile and swallowed back tears. But the truth is that at some point, I stopped feeling anything.

When we constantly shut down our feelings or pretend that everything is okay and live in other people's boxes, we just stop feeling anything. We stop having authentic relationships and connections. I was so concerned with my emotions being too much for people that I took away my own ability to be accepted, because I never let anyone know the truth of my pain or who I was. How many of us have lives that look so good on paper or in photos, but inside there's a part of us still aching? Social media makes this so easy to do with the pictures and activities that we think will look good to other people. The highlight reel of our lives posted for the world to see. It all looks so good on paper. But who does that benefit? We need to become a people who stop living a life that looks good on paper and start living a life that feels good on the inside. We need to live life out loud, not in the confines of what looks right to society or fits social norms.

So much of society lives with plastered-on smiles, pushing down pain, frustration, or anger, and trying to live a "good life" that looks right on paper. But is that how we're really called to live? When Jesus walked among us, he constantly broke what the religious leaders considered "religious law." He healed people on the Sabbath, He befriended those who others would not speak to. He called out hypocrites. Jesus did not live a life that looked good on paper. He associated with prostitutes, adulterers, and tax collectors. He called out the people who sat high and mighty preaching religious law, and yet, He is the One who lived a holy and righteous life. Because Jesus didn't just live a life that looked good on the outside; He lived a life that felt good and right on the inside. He listened to his heart and soul when they spoke to Him. He recognized anger and sadness as directional markers when they came up, and He didn't ignore them. He wept with the hurting. He got angry at the persecutors. He helped people who had a desire for change, and He rebuked those who believed they were above others and had lost sight of the heart of God.

I can't help but wonder what life would be like if we began to live a life that felt good on the inside, just as Jesus did. What would happen if we were true to our hearts and our emotions and spoke up when we felt something that hurt us? The more we push down our feelings and replace them with a smile, the less we feel. The more we pretend, the less anything is real. And the more we shut out the truth, the less we see it, even when it's in front of our faces. If we could just allow ourselves to feel more, maybe we could also be more open to see others hurting. Perhaps we'd better be able to recognize those around us who are holding on by a mere thread and on their way to a breakdown.

When we shut down our own emotions, we close ourselves off to our own hearts and souls and the Holy Spirit within us. We shut off our ears to the voice of God, and we close our eyes to the truth around us. We stop feeling the good moments as much as we stop feeling the hard ones. That is not living at all. Life is far too long to live a life that looks good but doesn't feel good, and it's far too short to go another day without making a change and taking a chance to live fully in truth and strive for a life that feels good on the inside. So, if you have lost something, take time to grieve and get sad and angry at the loss. If you are happy, laugh out loud, giggle, and be silly. If you are angry, express that anger in a healthy way and use it as a catalyst for change. Take time today to listen to your heart and listen to its desires. What do you want so much that you've been putting off? What have you been pretending is okay when it hurts? Is there a part of you that knows you aren't fulfilled, but has kept quiet? Who have you not spoken to in ages that you can reach out to and just catch up with? Give yourself nurturing love today and the permission to feel. Reach out to those around you in love. Look around and notice those who seem to be hurting. Hold the door for a stranger and smile genuinely at someone who needs it. Say the loving things that come to your mind. Listen to the still small voice in your heart. You never know what a difference the smallest of gestures can make. Don't live on paper; live out loud!

Reference Verses

Luke 6:22-23
What blessings await you when people hate you and exclude you and mock you and curse you as evil because you follow the Son of Man. When that happens, be happy! Yes, leap for joy! For a great reward awaits you in heaven. And remember, their ancestors treated the ancient prophets that same way.

Luke 13:10-17
One Sabbath day as Jesus was teaching in a synagogue, he saw a woman who had been crippled by an evil spirit. She had been bent double for eighteen years and was unable to stand up straight. When Jesus saw her, he called her over and said, "Dear woman, you are healed of your sickness!" Then he touched her, and instantly she could stand straight. How she praised God! But the leader in charge of the synagogue was indignant that Jesus had healed her on the Sabbath day. "There are six days of the week for working," he said to the crowd. "Come on those days to be healed, not on the Sabbath." But the Lord replied, "You hypocrites! Each of you works on the Sabbath day! Don't you untie your ox or your donkey from its stall on the Sabbath and lead it out for water? This dear woman, a daughter of Abraham, has been held in bondage by Satan for eighteen years. Isn't it right that she be released, even on the

Sabbath?" This shamed his enemies, but all the people rejoiced at the wonderful things he did.

Luke 15:1-7

Tax collectors and other notorious sinners often came to listen to Jesus teach. This made the Pharisees and teachers of religious law complain that he was associating with such sinful people—even eating with them! So Jesus told them this story: "If a man has a hundred sheep and one of them gets lost, what will he do? Won't he leave the ninety-nine others in the wilderness and go to search for the one that is lost until he finds it? And when he has found it, he will joyfully carry it home on his shoulders. When he arrives, he will call together his friends and neighbors, saying, 'Rejoice with me because I have found my lost sheep.' In the same way, there is more joy in heaven over one lost sinner who repents and returns to God than over ninety-nine others who are righteous and haven't strayed away!

John 9:13-16

Then they took the man who had been blind to the Pharisees, because it was on the Sabbath that Jesus had made the mud and healed him. The Pharisees asked the man all about it. So he told them, "He put the mud over my eyes, and when I washed it away, I could see!" Some of the Pharisees said, "This man Jesus is not from God, for he is working on the Sabbath." Others said, "But how could an ordinary sinner do such miraculous signs?" So there was a deep division of opinion among them.

John 16:13-15

When the Spirit of truth comes, he will guide you into all truth. He will not speak on his own but will tell you what he has heard. He will tell you about the future. He will bring me glory by telling you whatever he receives from me. All that belongs to the Father is mine; this is why I said, 'The Spirit will tell you whatever he receives from me.'

Matthew 5:3-11

"God blesses those who are poor and realize their need for him, for the Kingdom of Heaven is theirs. God blesses those who mourn, for they will be comforted. God blesses those who are humble, for they will inherit the whole earth. God blesses those who hunger and thirst for justice, for they will be satisfied. God blesses those who are merciful, for they will be shown mercy. God blesses those whose hearts are pure, for they will see God. God blesses those who work for peace, for they will be called the children of God. God blesses those who are persecuted for doing right, for the Kingdom of Heaven is theirs. God blesses you when people mock you and persecute you and lie about you and say all sorts of evil things against you because you are my followers. Be happy about it! Be very glad! For a great reward awaits you in heaven. And remember, the ancient prophets were persecuted in the same way.

Matthew 19:13-14

One day some parents brought their children to Jesus so he could lay his hands on them and pray for them. But the disciples scolded the parents for bothering him. But Jesus said, "Let the children come to me. Don't stop them! For the Kingdom of Heaven belongs to those who are like these children."

Matthew 23:12-15

But those who exalt themselves will be humbled, and those who humble themselves will be exalted. "What sorrow awaits you teachers of religious law and you Pharisees. Hypocrites! For you shut the door of the Kingdom of Heaven in people's faces. You won't go in yourselves, and you don't let others enter either. What sorrow awaits you teachers of religious law and you Pharisees. Hypocrites! For you cross land and sea to make one convert, and then you turn that person into twice the child of hell you yourselves are!"

Matthew 23:27-28

"What sorrow awaits you teachers of religious law and you Pharisees. Hypocrites! For you are like whitewashed tombs—beautiful on the outside but filled on the inside with dead people's bones and all sorts of impurity. Outwardly you look like righteous people, but inwardly your hearts are filled with hypocrisy and lawlessness."

Matthew 26:7-13

While he was eating, a woman came in with a beautiful alabaster jar of expensive perfume and poured it over his head. The disciples were indignant when they saw this. "What a waste!" they said. "It could have been sold for a high price and the money given to the poor." But Jesus, aware of this, replied, "Why criticize this woman for doing such a good thing to me? You will always have the poor among you, but you will not always have me. She has poured this perfume on me to prepare my body for burial. I tell you the truth, wherever the Good News is preached throughout the world, this woman's deed will be remembered and discussed."

Mark 3:1-5

Jesus went into the synagogue again and noticed a man with a deformed hand. Since it was the Sabbath, Jesus' enemies watched him closely. If he healed the man's hand, they planned to accuse him of working on the Sabbath. Jesus said to the man with the deformed hand, "Come and stand in front of everyone." Then he turned to his critics and asked, "Does the law permit good deeds on the Sabbath, or is it a day for doing evil? Is this a day to save life or to destroy it?" But they wouldn't answer him. He looked around at them angrily and was deeply saddened by their hard hearts. Then he said to the man, "Hold out your hand." So the man held out his hand, and it was restored!

Mark 7:5-8

So the Pharisees and teachers of religious law asked him, "Why don't your disciples follow our age-old tradition? They eat without first performing the hand-washing ceremony." Jesus replied, "You hypocrites! Isaiah was right when he prophesied about you, for he wrote, 'These people honor me with their lips, but their hearts are far from me. Their worship is a farce, for they teach man-made ideas as commands from God.' For you ignore God's law and substitute your own tradition."

John 11:33-35

When Jesus saw her weeping, and the jews who had come along with her also weeping, he was deeply moved in spirit and troubled. "Where have you laid him?" he asked. "Come and see, Lord," they replied. Jesus wept.

Mark 12:30-31

"And you must love the Lord your God with all your heart, all your soul, all your mind, and all your strength." The second is equally important: "Love your neighbor as yourself." No other commandment is greater than these."

Journal Space

_____

_____

_____

_____

_____

_____

Day 21:

Freedom

People often say, "Everybody, deep down, just wants to be loved." I do believe that this is true; however, perhaps love, in and of itself, is not really what people long for. Perhaps it's freedom. Freedom to love what and whom we desire, freedom to be fully ourselves without restraints, freedom to speak up when we see injustice, freedom to speak our hearts and express ourselves, freedom to be loved wholly and fully, freedom to not be abused, freedom from the weight of pain and hurt, freedom to not feel as though we have to walk on eggshells, freedom of privacy, freedom to have healthy, abundant relationships with friends and family, freedom to laugh, sing, cry, dance, be angry, be elated, to just be us: freedom.

If Christ died to set us free (Gal. 5:1) and "God is love" (1 John 4:8), then, perhaps, freedom can't exist without love and love can't exist without freedom. God—all powerful, almighty God—still gave us free will. He knew in all his wisdom that giving us free will also meant that we could deny Him. We could choose not to love Him, and we could choose not to receive His love, and yet, God still gives us this gift of choice. Why? Because God is love, and love cannot exist without freedom. No one can truly love, or truly be happy, if they are not free to choose.

So many people stay in abusive, painful, demeaning, and controlling situations because they believe that even if they don't feel happy, or free, self-sacrifice is part of love. Boundaries and freedom are often given up in the name of love, but I challenge that! That's not love at all; it's counterfeit. It's idolatry to put another so high up that you would give up the freedom that God gifted to you. When you are truly loved, you are free. When you truly love, you are free. Love never takes our freedom away or our right to choose. "Love does not insist on its own way." (1 Cor. 13:5 ESV). Freedom is an essential part of love and happiness. God, in all His glory and power, still gives us the right to choose. Don't ever be afraid to stand up for your wants, your needs, your boundaries, and your freedom. Have the courage to walk away from anything or anyone that doesn't give you freedom to be fully you. God made you just as you are for a reason. God knit you together in your mother's womb (Psalm 139:13) and he knew you before you were born (Jeremiah 1:5). You are not a mistake. You are precious to God. You are needed. If God loves us enough to give us the choice whether to follow Him and love Him or not, He surely gives you the choice to leave an unhappy, unhealthy situation as well, regardless of any promises that may have been made.

There are times in our lives when we have made the wrong choices. We may have even made choices that seemed right at the time, but they led to brokenness, pain, and unrest. We aren't all-knowing. We aren't God. There will be times when we end up taking the wrong path, making promises to the wrong people, and ending up in the wrong relationships, or at the wrong destinations, because we do have free will. We will not always choose right. But just as God gave us the free will to choose our original path, which may have led to pain, He also gave us the right to change our minds, to turn around, to make a different choice. At any given moment, we have the right to choose. The devil has no power to take God's blessings from you, but you can forfeit them out of fear and guilt, just as you can forfeit your freedom. Freedom is a God-given human right. Christ died so that we could live abundantly and free; don't diminish what Christ did for us on the cross by giving up the gift of freedom that He gave you.

Reference Verses

Psalm 119:45 NIV
I will walk about in freedom, for I have sought out your precepts.

Psalm 139:13 NIV
For you created my inmost being; you knit me together in my mother's womb.

Jeremiah 1:5 NIV
"Before I formed you in the womb I knew you, before you were born I set you apart; I appointed you as a prophet to the nations."

Isaiah 61:1 NIV
The Spirit of the Sovereign Lord is on me, because the Lord has anointed me to proclaim good news to the poor. He has sent me to bind up the brokenhearted, to proclaim freedom for the captives and release from darkness for the prisoners

1 Corinthians 6:12 NIV
"I have the right to do anything," you say—but not everything is beneficial. "I have the right to do anything"—but I will not be mastered by anything.

1 Corinthians 13:4-6

Love is patient and kind. Love is not jealous or boastful or proud or rude. It does not demand its own way. It is not irritable, and it keeps no record of being wronged. It does not rejoice about injustice but rejoices whenever the truth wins out.

2 Timothy 2:26 ESV

And they may come to their senses and escape from the snare of the devil, after being captured by him to do his will.

2 Corinthians 3:16-17 NIV

But whenever anyone turns to the Lord, the veil is taken away. Now the Lord is the Spirit, and where the Spirit of the Lord is, there is freedom.

2 Corinthians 11:14-15 NIV

And no wonder, for Satan himself masquerades as an angel of light. It is not surprising, then, if his servants also masquerade as servants of righteousness. Their end will be what their actions deserve.

John 8:36 NIV

So if the Son sets you free, you will be free indeed.

John 10:10 NIV

The thief comes only to steal and kill and destroy; I have come that they may have life, and have it to the full.

1 John 4:7-8 NIV

Dear friends, let us love one another, for love comes from God. Everyone who loves has been born of God and knows God. Whoever does not love does not know God, because God is love.

Galatians 2:4 NIV

This matter arose because some false believers had infiltrated our ranks to spy on the freedom we have in Christ Jesus and to make us slaves.

Galatians 2:19-21 NIV

"For through the law I died to the law so that I might live for God. I have been crucified with Christ and I no longer live, but Christ lives in me. The life I now live in the body, I live by faith in the Son of God, who loved me and gave himself for me. I do not set aside the grace of God, for if righteousness could be gained through the law, Christ died for nothing!"

Galatians 4:3-5

And that's the way it was with us before Christ came. We were like children; we were slaves to the basic spiritual principles of this world. But when the right time came, God sent his Son, born of a woman, subject to the law. God sent him to buy freedom for us who were slaves to the law, so that he could adopt us as his very own children.

Galatians 5:1 NIV

It is for freedom that Christ has set us free. Stand firm, then, and do not let yourselves be burdened again by a yoke of slavery.

Ephesians 3:12 NIV

In him and through faith in him we may approach God with freedom and confidence.

Luke 4:18 NIV

The Spirit of the Lord is on me, because he has anointed me to proclaim good news to the poor. He has sent me to proclaim freedom for the prisoners and recovery of sight for the blind, to set the oppressed free

Journal Space

_____

_____

_____

_____

_____

_____

Day 22:

Tread with Love

One of my favorite verses in the Bible says, "There is no fear in love; but perfect love casts out fear, because fear involves torment. But he who fears has not been made perfect in love." (1 John 4:18 NKJV). Let's be honest, not one of us has been made perfect in love. We all face fears at some point. Will I be able to pay my bills? What is going to happen with my job? Is my relationship okay? Will I be stuck in this place forever? I can't afford to be sick, what if I get sick? Life is riddled with unknowns, and what ifs. It's covered in uncertainty, and it's not black and white. We will inevitably face fears and have anxiety. However, just because we face fear doesn't mean we have to be overcome by it. Facing fear doesn't mean we are supposed to stop giving love or moving forward. So, what does it mean to tread with love? It means move forward in love; don't let fear paralyze you. Speak your truth, even if your mouth runs dry and your voice shakes. Know that your wants, your desires, your loves, are worth fighting for, worth speaking up about, worth the risk. Keep moving forward in love at all times. Trust that love will never steer you wrong.

There is a lot we can't control in this life. In truth, we can't control anything except what we choose to put out into the world. I choose love. I know that no matter what happens around me, no matter what anyone does or doesn't do, as long as I have gone forward in love, been true to myself, and given as much love as I can, I have done all I can do. I have done my part.

When you've done all you can do, just stand. To stand doesn't mean halting. It doesn't mean holding back. It means showing up. It means being consistent. It means giving love. And when we've done all we can do, that's when God shows up and does what He can do. For His strength is made perfect in our weaknesses. I don't want to reach the end of the road and look back and wonder what would have happened if I had just chosen to fight through my fears, and show my heart, and give my love. When we choose love, miracles happen.

Choosing love might not mean that everyone we come across is good to us, or that they know how to receive our love, or give anything back. And it certainly doesn't mean that we should stay in situations or relationships in which we are being hurt in the name of love. That is not love at all. What it means is that we are true to ourselves and don't hold ourselves, or our vulnerabilities, back out of fear. It means that we can look back and know that we did our part, and maybe, the love that we gave will make a difference in the future.

Regardless of whether we ever see how our love has affected others, it always makes a difference for us. Because when you deny yourself, your truth, or your heart, there is a part of you that shuts down. No one can live a healthy, happy, effective, Godly life if they constantly shut down their own needs, wants, desires, and loves. We need to nurture our own needs if we are to have anything left to give to others. When we live and walk in love, we live in integrity—where our hearts, our minds, and our actions resonate as one. Treading with love is being true to your soul. It's reminding your heart that you have a voice and that voice matters. It means not allowing fear or guilt to kill, steal, and destroy the goodness that God brings into your life. "Tread with love" is a phrase that echoes in my heart as a constant reminder to not shut down out of fear and make a conscious choice daily to walk in love. How will you walk?

Reference Verses

Proverbs 27:5
An open rebuke is better than hidden love.

Song of Songs 8:7
Many waters cannot quench love, nor can rivers drown it. If a man tried to buy love with all his wealth, his offer would be utterly scorned.

1 John 4:16-18 NIV
And so we know and rely on the love God has for us. God is love. Whoever lives in love lives in God, and God in them. This is how love is made complete among us so that we will have confidence on the Day of Judgment: In this world we are like Jesus. There is no fear in love. But perfect love drives out fear, because fear has to do with punishment. The one who fears is not made perfect in love.

2 John 1:6 NIV
And this is love: that we walk in obedience to his commands. As you have heard from the beginning, his command is that you walk in love.

1 Corinthians 13
If I could speak all the languages of earth and of angels, but didn't love others, I would only be a noisy gong or a clanging cymbal. If I had the gift of prophecy, and if I understood all of God's secret plans and possessed all knowledge, and if I had such faith that I could move mountains, but

didn't love others, I would be nothing. If I gave everything I have to the poor and even sacrificed my body, I could boast about it; but if I didn't love others, I would have gained nothing. Love is patient and kind. Love is not jealous or boastful or proud or rude. It does not demand its own way. It is not irritable, and it keeps no record of being wronged. It does not rejoice about injustice but rejoices whenever the truth wins out. Love never gives up, never loses faith, is always hopeful, and endures through every circumstance. Prophecy and speaking in unknown languages and special knowledge will become useless. But love will last forever!

Ephesians 4:14-16

Then we will no longer be immature like children. We won't be tossed and blown about by every wind of new teaching. We will not be influenced when people try to trick us with lies so clever they sound like the truth. Instead, we will speak the truth in love, growing in every way more and more like Christ, who is the head of his body, the church. He makes the whole body fit together perfectly. As each part does its own special work, it helps the other parts grow, so that the whole body is healthy and growing and full of love.

2 John 1:3

Grace, mercy, and peace, which come from God the Father and from Jesus Christ—the Son of the Father—will continue to be with us who live in truth and love.

1 Corinthians 16:13-14

Be on guard. Stand firm in the faith. Be courageous. Be strong. And do everything with love.

Galatians 5:6

For when we place our faith in Christ Jesus, there is no benefit in being circumcised or being uncircumcised. What is important is faith expressing itself in love.

Colossians 3:14

Above all, clothe yourselves with love, which binds us all together in perfect harmony.

Journal Space

_____

_____

_____

_____

_____

_____

Day 23:

Dark and Light

Night and day, dark and light, good and evil—our world is full of contrast. We all experience both sides of the spectrum, and yet, each person leans one way or the other. Some of us live in the light and relish it. The light feels warm and comforting and it fills us with hope. The shadow of darkness is cold and terrifying. Some of us live right on the line, fearing the light, afraid that if we step into it fully, we will be exposed. But we're still cold and sick at the feeling of darkness, in limbo, afraid that if we step into the light, our broken, fettered pieces will be on display. So, we stand on the line, barely enjoying the sunshine for fear of exposure, but longing for the warmth. Some people live in darkness. Maybe they were raised in darkness and it feels so normal that the warmth of the sun sears their skin and causes them to retreat. Maybe they enjoy the darkness, hiding in the cool comfort of their own unhappiness and entitlement. They avoid the light at all costs, because if they were to face it, it would expose their hearts—the bitterness, the anger, and the resentment. It would expose the lies, the destruction, and the pain. Pain that they refuse to take responsibility for. Pain they refuse to accept, and pain they refuse to change. Every choice they make pulls them deeper into the abyss, because that's where they feel comfortable, surrounded by a blanket of night. We are all faced with a choice: darkness or light. We all either choose to live in a closed box of darkness or free in the sunshine. Living in the light means vulnerability. Living in the light means compassion and empathy and love. Living in the light means exposure. But, when one lives in integrity, they don't care how visible they are to the world, or how brightly the light shines on each perfect imperfection. Living in the light does not mean that night never falls, but it means that even in the dark, they look up at the stars. The cool of shadows still graze their skin in moments, as the shade of a tree covers them, but they still know that it's the very light that casts the shadow, and they still look up. They may pass through a tunnel, but they always see the light shining at the end, and no matter how dark a moment seems around them, they move to the light. The whisper in their hearts is no longer a whisper, but an out-loud song—a song they sing to the world shamelessly, because their hearts and their minds, and their actions all meet. Integrity is the solid ground on which they stand. Nothing is hidden, because nothing has to be.

Each one of us has at least grazed both the dark and the light of life. But it's always our choice. Have you been living in a tight, dark box? Has it felt comfortable, unexposed to the elements? Maybe you've grazed the line, afraid of the exposure the sun has to offer, but longing for the warmth of it on your face. We all have a choice each and every day: to lean toward the darkness or to follow the light and stand unashamed in it's warm presence, completely exposed and completely free.

Reference Verses

Proverbs 10:9 NIV
Whoever walks in integrity walks securely, but whoever takes crooked paths will be found out.

1 John 1:6-7 NIV

If we claim to have fellowship with him and yet walk in the darkness, we lie and do not live out the truth. But if we walk in the light, as he is in the light, we have fellowship with one another, and the blood of Jesus, his Son, purifies us from all sin. (NIV)

John 3:20-21 NIV

Everyone who does evil hates the light, and will not come into the light for fear that their deeds will be exposed. But whoever lives by the truth comes into the light, so that it may be seen plainly that what they have done has been done in the sight of God. (NIV)

Luke 8:16-17 NIV

No one lights a lamp and hides it in a clay jar or puts it under a bed. Instead, they put it on a stand, so that those who come in can see the light. For there is nothing hidden that will not be disclosed, and nothing concealed that will not be known or brought out into the open.

Luke 11:33-36 NIV

No one lights a lamp and puts it in a place where it will be hidden, or under a bowl. Instead they put it on its stand, so that those who come in may see the light. Your eye is the lamp of your body. When your eyes are healthy, your whole body also is full of light. But when they are unhealthy, your body also is full of darkness. See to it, then, that the light within you is not darkness. Therefore, if your whole body is full of light, and no part of it dark, it will be just as full of light as when a lamp shines its light on you.

Matthew 10:26-31 NIV

So do not be afraid of them, for there is nothing concealed that will not be disclosed, or hidden that will not be made known. What I tell you in the dark, speak in the daylight; what is whispered in your ear, proclaim from the roofs. Do not be afraid of those who kill the body but cannot kill the soul. Rather, be afraid of the One who can destroy both soul and body in hell. Are not two sparrows sold for a penny? Yet not one of them will fall to the ground outside your Father's care. And even the very hairs of your head are all numbered. So don't be afraid; you are worth more than many sparrows.

(See also related Luke 12:2-9)

Ephesians 5:8-14 NIV

For you were once darkness, but now you are light in the Lord. Live as children of light (for the fruit of the light consists in all goodness, righteousness and truth) and find out what pleases the Lord. Have nothing to do with the fruitless deeds of darkness, but rather expose them. It is shameful even to mention what the disobedient do in secret. But everything exposed by the light becomes visible—and everything that is illuminated becomes a light. This is why it is said: "Wake up, sleeper, rise from the dead, and Christ will shine on you."

Romans 13:12 NIV

The night is nearly over; the day is almost here. So let us put aside the deeds of darkness and put on the armor of light.

1 Thessalonians 5:5-6 NIV

You are all children of the light and children of the day. We do not belong to the night or to the darkness. So then, let us not be like others, who are asleep, but let us be awake and sober.

Acts 13:47 NIV

For this is what the Lord has commanded us: "'I have made you a light for the Gentiles, that you may bring salvation to the ends of the earth.'"

Journal Space

_____

_____

_____

_____

_____

_____

Day 24:

Magic of Spring

There is something about Spring—the birds singing a jovial melody, flitting back and forth to attend to their nests, the smells of soft, sweet blossoms wafting through the air, green leaves and flowers, like puffs of snow, pink and white decorate the trees, the sun warming your skin. There's a release of sorts, like the suspension of winter is going back into motion. Spring: the season of hope. The season that reminds us that no matter how dark, how cold, and how colorless our world gets, there is always a spring, a rebirth, a warming, a bursting of color and life. From the winter always comes the spring.

There is something about spring that gives me a sense of comfort and joy in my spirit. It shows up, almost like a guarantee that things will be okay, that the sun will shine again and warmth will fill your heart. No matter what I'm going through, it's hard not to feel a sense of hope and anticipation in springtime—anticipation of the good and exciting things that are coming, as if they are inevitable. I become like a child on a treasure hunt, exploring every turn with pleasure and excitement of what gem may lie right around the next bend.

We all have seasons in our lives, falls where things are falling and dying away, winters where everything seems to be frozen and dark, but we also all have springs, where rebirth and fresh life begins. No matter what you are going through in life—personally, workwise, or health-wise—just know that this moment has treasure in it. There is something magical to be discovered right where you are if you show up and look with anticipation, and even if you are going through a personal winter, there will always be a spring, if you just hang on. I hope you go outside this week and enjoy the changing world around you. I hope that you notice the shifting colors, that you stop to listen to the birds singing, and close your eyes and feel the sun on your face. Feel this and know that better days are coming, and there is treasure and magic right where you are!

Reference Verses

Genesis 8:22 NIV
As long as the earth endures, seedtime and harvest, cold and heat, summer and winter, day and night will never cease.

Psalm 1:2-3 NIV
But whose delight is in the law of the Lord, and who meditates on his law day and night. That person is like a tree planted by streams of water, which yields its fruit in season and whose leaf does not wither—whatever they do prospers.

Isaiah 55:10-11 NIV
As the rain and the snow come down from heaven, and do not return to it without watering the earth and making it bud and flourish, so that it yields seed for the sower and bread for the eater, so is my word that goes out from my mouth: It will not return to me empty, but will accomplish what I desire and achieve the purpose for which I sent it.

Song of Songs 2:11-13 NIV

See! The winter is past; the rains are over and gone. Flowers appear on the earth; the season of singing has come, the cooing of doves is heard in our land. The fig tree forms its early fruit; the blossoming vines spread their fragrance. Arise, come, my darling; my beautiful one, come with me.

Ezekiel 34:26 NIV

I will make them and the places surrounding my hill a blessing. I will send down showers in season; there will be showers of blessing.

Ecclesiastes 3:1-22 NIV

There is a time for everything, and a season for every activity under the heavens: a time to be born and a time to die, a time to plant and a time to uproot, a time to kill and a time to heal, a time to tear down and a time to build, a time to weep and a time to laugh, a time to mourn and a time to dance, a time to scatter stones and a time to gather them, a time to embrace and a time to refrain from embracing, a time to search and a time to give up, a time to keep and a time to throw away, a time to tear and a time to mend, a time to be silent and a time to speak, a time to love and a time to hate, a time for war and a time for peace. What do workers gain from their toil? I have seen the burden God has laid on the human race. He has made everything beautiful in its time. He has also set eternity in the human heart; yet no one can fathom what God has done from beginning to end. I know that there is nothing better for people than to be happy and to do good while they live. That each of them may eat and drink, and find satisfaction in all their toil—this is the gift of God. I know that everything God does will endure forever; nothing can be added to it and nothing taken from it. God does it so that people will fear him.

Galatians 6:9 NIV

Let us not become weary in doing good, for at the proper time we will reap a harvest if we do not give up.

Matthew 24:32 NIV

Now learn this lesson from the fig tree: As soon as its twigs get tender and its leaves come out, you know that summer is near.

2 Timothy 4:2 NIV

Preach the word; be prepared in season and out of season; correct, rebuke and encourage—with great patience and careful instruction.

1 Peter 1:6-9 NIV

In all this you greatly rejoice, though now for a little while you may have had to suffer grief in all kinds of trials. These have come so that the proven genuineness of your faith—of greater worth than gold, which perishes even though refined by fire—may result in praise, glory and honor when Jesus Christ is revealed. Though you have not seen him, you love him; and even though you do not see him now, you believe in him and are filled with an inexpressible and glorious joy, for you are receiving the end result of your faith, the salvation of your souls.

Journal Space

_____

_____

_____

_____

_____

_____

Day 25:

God's Faithfulness

There are times in life that are an exercise in patience. Times when it seems like no matter what we do, there's another hurdle waiting for us, another piece of bad news, another shoe ready to drop. Times when we feel like we have to just keep moving to survive, but we're exhausted. Times when nothing is easy, relationships are struggling, finances are on the edge, and nothing seems certain or settled. Life can be feast or famine. It can feel like running a marathon where the finish line keeps getting moved farther away, and you barely have the strength to keep moving. We've all dealt with disappointments, pain, and frustration, and sometimes it can feel like we will never reach the finish line and there is no end in sight. It's moments like these when we need to just take one step at a time, one day at a time. When life seems overwhelming, it's not about what you have to do in a month, or even a day, but what you have to do today to keep moving forward, to keep having faith. Sometimes we become so focused on the finish line that we forget it's the journey along the way that really counts.

In moments of overwhelm, we have to remind ourselves of God's faithfulness in the past. We have to remember His faithfulness, not just in big things, but also in little things—in moments, in signs, in a friendly smile, or in a good conversation. We need to remember moments when He takes what you've gone through and enables you to bless someone else with understanding, moments when a stranger makes your day with the right word at the right time. Take one day at a time, one moment at a time, living and breathing through each. Feel the ground under your feet, look at what's right in front of you, and be present. Remember God's faithfulness in your past, to bring fulfillment and to bring closure, to help propel you forward. What times did God use even the hardship, even the things that hurt, to bring good in other ways? Know that God has started a good work in you, and he will be faithful to fulfill it. (Phil. 1:6). If something feels unfinished, or unsettled, or unfulfilled, it is. It is not finished yet, and God is still working. It's not over until God says it's over.

Reference Verses

Jeremiah 29:11 NIV
"For I know the plans I have for you," declares the Lord, "plans to prosper you and not to harm you, plans to give you hope and a future."

Joshua 21:45
Not a single one of all the good promises the Lord had given to the family of Israel was left unfulfilled; everything he had spoken came true.

Isaiah 25:1 NIV
Lord, you are my God; I will exalt you and praise your name, for in perfect faithfulness you have done wonderful things, things planned long ago.

Deuteronomy 7:9 NIV

Know therefore that the Lord your God is God; he is the faithful God, keeping his covenant of love to a thousand generations of those who love him and keep his commandments.

Numbers 23:19 NIV

God is not human, that he should lie, not a human being, that he should change his mind. Does he speak and then not act? Does he promise and not fulfill?

2 Timothy 2:13 NIV

If we are faithless, He remains faithful, for He cannot disown himself.

2 Thessalonians 3:3 NIV

But the Lord is faithful, and he will strengthen you and protect you from the evil one.

Psalm 33:4-5 NIV

For the word of the Lord is right and true; he is faithful in all he does. The Lord loves righteousness and justice; the earth is full of his unfailing love.

Psalm 36:5-6 NIV

Your love, Lord, reaches to the heavens, your faithfulness to the skies. Your righteousness is like the highest mountains, your justice like the great deep. You, Lord, preserve both people and animals.

Hebrews 10:22-23 NIV

Let us draw near to God with a sincere heart and with the full assurance that faith brings, having our hearts sprinkled to cleanse us from a guilty conscience and having our bodies washed with pure water. Let us hold unswervingly to the hope we profess, for he who promised is faithful.

Hebrews 11:1-3 NIV

Now faith is confidence in what we hope for and assurance about what we do not see. This is what the ancients were commended for. By faith we understand that the universe was formed at God's command, so that what is seen was not made out of what was visible.

Hebrews 11:11 NIV

And by faith even Sarah, who was past childbearing age, was enabled to bear children because she considered Him faithful who had made the promise.

Philippians 1:6

And I am certain that God, who began the good work within you, will continue his work until it is finally finished on the day when Christ Jesus returns.

Romans 3:3-4 NIV

What if some were unfaithful? Will their unfaithfulness nullify God's faithfulness? Not at all! Let God be true, and every human being a liar. As it is written: "So that you may be proved right when you speak and prevail when you judge."

Journal Space

_____
_____
_____
_____
_____
_____

Day 26:

The Emerging Butterfly

The pressure was mounting. Each day more tension built as the chrysalis grew tighter around her growing wings. There was a sense of the light, a sense of the day time, a warming, the heat pouring into the tight, cramped space, like a reminder of the daylight, of the fresh air, of the grass tickling her feet. But still, she sat in treacherous darkness. And every day that passed, the space got smaller, the pressure built, like the weight of the world was surrounding her, she felt like there was nowhere to go, no way to turn. She barely had the strength to breathe … Free … She wanted to break free, to feel the breeze on her face once again, to see the flowers and trees, dancing like fairies in the wind. She wanted to smell the sweet caressing scent of roses and feel the soft cushion of their petals. Free. The tension built to the point that she could take it no longer. With the last ounce of strength she had left, she pressed, she pushed, she wiggled—anything to break free! She knew she'd either break free or die trying, because the pain of staying bound in the chrysalis was too much. Rage, anguish, but mostly hope, a divine energy filled her as she pressed mightily against the walls that bound her. The first sign of fresh air almost went unnoticed, as she struggled to bust through the binding. But then, a cool breeze raced by, and the immediate relief of the cool air against her body sent excitement through her and gave her renewed strength. Almost there! The binding was losing its grip on her, the tension started to fall away. She was almost out. And in a moment, after great courage and strength, release! She broke through. The sun shone its rays of warmth down her body, and she looked up to soak it in. She went to stretch her body, but something felt different. She looked down, expecting to see herself as she was before she'd been bound, but there was no caterpillar in sight. Instead, there stood a beautiful butterfly with outspread wings of golden spots. The breeze blew again and lifted her up into its currents, the sun danced on her face and reflected off her wings, and she had the most glorious view of the world. Better than she'd remembered it.

How often in our lives are we the butterfly? Tested by dark and binding circumstances, feeling the heat turned up, but seeing no sign of light. How often do we feel bound and lose our strength? Life turns up the heat, and God puts us in chrysalises of our own at times, knowing that once we get fed up with the tension, once the pressure has mounted enough, we will grow a beautiful pair of wings and break free from the confines of who we used to be. Free of old scripts that played in our heads and held us back, of poor habits, of negative people. More importantly, we will grow into beautiful, grateful, golden, shining souls. The ones with golden wings who have tasted the darkness, felt it creep up on us, and refused to let it win. Because it is the golden wings that we grew that reflect the light of the sun to others.

Reference Verses

Psalm 66:10-12 NASB

For you have tried us, O God; You have refined us as silver is refined. You brought us into the net; You laid an oppressive burden upon our loins You made men ride over our heads; We went through fire and through water. Yet you brought us out into a place of abundance.

Psalm 34:18
The Lord is close to the brokenhearted; he rescues those whose spirits are crushed.

Proverbs 30:1
I am weary, O God; I am weary and worn out, O God.

1 Samuel 2:8
He lifts the poor from the dust and the needy from the garbage dump. He sets them among princes, placing them in seats of honor. For all the earth is the Lord's, and he has set the world in order.

Isaiah 40:31 NIV
But those who hope in the Lord will renew their strength. They will soar on wings like eagles; they will run and not grow weary, they will walk and not be faint.

Isaiah 43:2
When you go through deep waters, I will be with you. When you go through rivers of difficulty, you will not drown. When you walk through the fire of oppression, you will not be burned up; the flames will not consume you.

Mark 9:23
"What do you mean, 'If I can'?" Jesus asked. "Anything is possible if a person believes."

Matthew 17:20

"You don't have enough faith," Jesus told them. "I tell you the truth, if you had faith even as small as a mustard seed, you could say to this mountain, 'Move from here to there,' and it would move. Nothing would be impossible."

Ephesians 3:20-21 NIV

Now to him who is able to do immeasurably more than all we ask or imagine, according to his power that is at work within us, to him be glory in the church and in Christ Jesus throughout all generations, for ever and ever! Amen.

2 Corinthians 5:17 NIV

Therefore, if anyone is in Christ, the new creation has come: The old has gone, the new is here!

2 Corinthians 3:18

So all of us who have had that veil removed can see and reflect the glory of the Lord. And the Lord—who is the spirit—makes us more and more like him as we are changed into his glorious image.

Philippians 1:6 NIV

Being confident of this, that he who began a good work in you will carry it on to completion until the day of Christ Jesus.

1 Peter 5:10

In his kindness, God called you to share in his eternal glory by means of Christ Jesus. So after you have suffered a little while, he will restore, support, and strengthen you, and he will place you on a firm foundation.

Philippians 3:21 NIV
Who, by the power that enables him to bring everything under his control, will transform our lowly bodies so that they will be like his glorious body.

Journal Space

_____

_____

_____

_____

_____

_____

Day 27:

Collateral Blessings

There are some things in life that just don't make sense. There are some hurts that don't just heal or get better. When you lose a loved one to death, for example, you don't get to be with them every day—not in this life—and missing them hurts. My grandfather died when I was seven years old. I still cry when I see pictures of him. I still wish he were here to talk to when life gets crazy. There is a part of grieving that hangs on. People like to say that what doesn't kill you makes you stronger, but this isn't true. There are some hurts that weaken us, that break down our self-esteem, that tamper with our faith, that harden our spirits. Trauma doesn't always strengthen; sometimes it harms. Sometimes it puts out our light or makes the load we are carrying seem so heavy that it feels like we will topple under the weight. A little over three years ago, I was diagnosed with PTSD (Post Traumatic Stress Disorder). I had never been to war. I had never witnessed acts of extreme violence. The trauma that I had experienced was relational. It was death, it was abuse, it was stalking and threats. It wasn't a big, traumatic incident; it was layers that added up over time until my nervous system couldn't take the load and started reacting. Something simple could happen in everyday life and I would be triggered and suddenly feel like I had lost everything and was grieving. It felt like the world was caving in. Even when things were going well, it seemed I was always waiting for the other shoe to drop and tentatively looking at the sky in hopes it wouldn't hit me if I ducked fast enough.

If you have trauma in your past, it can be so hard to see God's goodness at work, and even harder to believe that things will get better or that He is faithful. When your faith is tested and you go through trials, people often tell you to look back and remember what God has done, but when your past is laden with trauma, looking back doesn't always boost your faith. In fact, sometimes it hinders it. Because, when you look back, you see the trauma, you see the pain, and you see the darkness that you are frantically trying to crawl out of. It can be hard to see any light, any hope, any goodness in moments of total overwhelm, when you can't see the future clearly, the past looks dark and the present hurts. But these are the moments you have to strain to find the blessings in the midst of the pain, the little things that show God's goodness.

We are not promised that this life will be easy. In fact, we know we will face many trials and much suffering in this life. But we are promised, "after you have suffered a little while, He will restore, support, and strengthen you, and he will place you on a firm foundation." (1 Peter 5:10). We are made another promise as well, a promise that some days I have to meditate on over and over, until my heart believes that it is true. We are promised that God works all things together for our good. (Romans 8:28). This doesn't mean some things; this means *all* things. This means that even the things that God did not will—even our mistakes—He can use for the greater good, and even for our personal good long-term.

Not everything that happens in this life is God's will. There are two things at play here. 1) We have an enemy that is a spirit too, and he tries to invade our thoughts and lie to us about ourselves. The enemy doesn't want us to be free, and he comes dressed as an angel of light to confuse us when a breakthrough is near. 2) We have free will, and sometimes we make choices that aren't God's best for us. It doesn't mean we are bad people, or even that we have bad intentions. In fact, sometimes bad choices come masquerading as things we think we are supposed to do, things that seem right. Perhaps the enemy has confused us with guilt and shame and caused us to believe we are bound to something or someone, that it is our duty. Regardless of what the reason is, there are times we end up on a path that God did not will for us, and it hurts. But, as promised in His word, he can and does use even those things to work together for our good. He can take what the enemy intended for our harm and use it for our good. This is most evidenced in collateral blessings.

Collateral blessings often aren't the big breakthroughs that you pray for and wait for. They are the small things along the way that keep you going. They are the dear friends you wouldn't have met on a different path. They are the small wins, the quiet moments with loved ones, the epiphanies you have that bring you a new level of freedom or understanding. You see, not everything we go through makes us stronger; some things make us weaker, but God is made great in our weakness. God can use even that weakness, even our hurt, to do good in our lives and the lives of others. When we are hurt, we gain compassion and understanding for other people's pain. God uses this. Think about moments when God has placed you in places and with people who needed your understanding, your tender heart, because they were going through something you once walked through. Collateral blessings are the moments you get to give the gift of yourself to another person, the moments when God sends you a message, telling you He's still there and still working for you. Collateral blessings are the people who come into your life to encourage you and offer understanding when you are hurting. Collateral blessings are the things you learn along the way that help you to the next step. Collateral blessings are the answered silent prayers and the moments of reprieve while you are going through a hardship. Collateral blessings are all the ways God can use what you are going through for good, both in your life and in the lives of other people. There is beauty even in the pain; sometimes we just have to look deeper to find it. But know this: no matter how hard it seems at times, the Lord's plans for you are good. He has "Plans to prosper you, and not to harm you, plans to give you hope and a future." (Jeremiah 29:11 NIV). You still have hope for a good and prosperous future. Believe! Keep moving, keep trusting, and keep looking for the collateral blessings.

Reference Verses

Lamentations 3:22-23
The faithful love of the Lord never ends! His mercies never cease. Great is his faithfulness; his mercies begin afresh each morning.

Deuteronomy 7:8-9
Rather, it was simply that the Lord loves you, and he was keeping the oath he had sworn to your ancestors. That is why the Lord rescued you with such a strong hand from your slavery and from the oppressive hand of Pharaoh, king of Egypt. Understand, therefore, that the Lord your God is indeed God. He is the faithful God who keeps his covenant for a thousand generations and lavishes his unfailing love on those who love him and obey his commands.

1 Kings 8:56
Praise the Lord who has given rest to his people Israel, just as he promised. Not one word has failed of all the wonderful promises he gave through his servant Moses.

Psalm 106:7-8

Our ancestors in Egypt were not impressed by the Lord's miraculous deeds. They soon forgot his many acts of kindness to them. Instead, they rebelled against him at the Red Sea. Even so, he saved them to defend the honor of his name and to demonstrate his mighty power.

Jeremiah 29:11

"For I know the plans I have for you," says the Lord. "They are plans for good and not for disaster, to give you a future and a hope."

Joshua 23:14

Soon I will die, going the way of everything on earth. Deep in your hearts you know that every promise of the Lord your God has come true. Not a single one has failed!

Romans 8:28

And we know that God causes everything to work together for the good of those who love God and are called according to his purpose for them.

2 Corinthians 12:9

Each time he said, "My grace is all you need. My power works best in weakness." So now I am glad to boast about my weaknesses, so that the power of Christ can work through me.

2 Timothy 2:13

If we are unfaithful, he remains faithful, for he cannot deny who he is.

Romans 4:20-22

Abraham never wavered in believing God's promise. In fact, his faith grew stronger, and in this he brought glory to God. He was fully convinced that God is able to do whatever he promises. And because of Abraham's faith, God counted him as righteous.

1 Thessalonians 5:24

God will make this happen, for he who calls you is faithful.

1 Peter 5:10

In his kindness God called you to share in his eternal glory by means of Christ Jesus. So after you have suffered a little while, he will restore, support, and strengthen you, and he will place you on a firm foundation.

Journal Space

_____

_____

_____

_____

_____

_____

Day 28:

Anticipation

There are times when we pray and the answer doesn't come right away. There are seasons of waiting, when it feels like we've been walking in a valley for so long that we aren't sure if there is a way out, or if we'll ever reach the mountaintop that we have prayed so fervently for. It is so easy to feel stagnant in times of waiting. It can feel like life is suddenly at a standstill and nothing will change until you receive your breakthrough. But the truth is that there is growth in the waiting. There are times when God doesn't just call us to wait, but He calls us to wait with anticipation. We are to anticipate the breakthroughs we have been praying for, the healing, the blessing, the restoration, and the provision. We are to believe in the things we pray for and wait for them with excitement and anticipation, and know that even if it takes time, God is still working, and we are still preparing for our blessing.

It can be scary to wait with anticipation when we don't see God working behind the scenes. Because in our world, when we anticipate something, it usually occurs pretty immediately. Perhaps it's the laughter you anticipate after a joke, or the friends who are arriving from out of town you anticipate coming. We live in a world of instant gratification, but God's timeframe is different than ours. It can be scary to anticipate something, not knowing when it will come to pass. We fear disappointment. We fear that if we hope for something and it doesn't come, we will get hurt. But what does God say about faith? God says that if you have the faith of a mustard seed, you can move mountains (Matthew 17:20). With faith, you can walk on water. But it is easy to doubt the power of faith when we are caught up in our circumstances. In one story in the Bible, when Peter saw Jesus on the water, he immediately stepped out of the boat, to go to Jesus and embrace him, and he walked on water, because he was looking at God. However, as soon as Peter stopped looking at God and looked at the water around him, he started to sink (Matthew 14:28-31). We do this to ourselves when we take our eyes off God and His promises to us.

It is easy to falter in our faith when we don't see immediate changes or answers to our prayers. It is hard to anticipate blessings when days stretch into months, and months sometimes stretch into years, and yet God's timing is not our timing. God Promised Abraham that he would be the father to all nations and have many descendants (Genesis 17:2-4). Abraham believed God and waited with anticipation until he felt that God's promise was taking too long, and he felt he had to take matters into his own hands. Abraham forgot that, to God, time means nothing, and age is not a limit, so he impregnated his housekeeper instead of his wife (Genesis 16:1-4), believing that this was the only way to receive God's promise. He settled for less than what God had for him. Luckily for Abraham, God had other plans. When Abraham was one hundred years old, God fulfilled His promise, just as He said He would; it just wasn't in a timeframe that Abraham could have ever imagined.

If God's timing is so different from ours, what does it mean to wait with anticipation? How do we wait and keep heart? We must anticipate, without expecting it to happen in a particular way, or in a particular time frame. And we must prepare for our blessings. You see, it may feel like we are stuck or stagnant in times of waiting, but the truth is that even in times of waiting, God doesn't want us to stop moving. He calls us to keep moving, and growing, and learning, and preparing for the blessings that we have been praying for. When a weight lifter trains for competition, he doesn't go from lifting twenty-pound weights, to lifting five-hundred-pound weights. Even if it were possible for him, jumping to the heavy weights would result in injuries and possibly even prevent him from being able to compete long-term. In order to prepare for competition, a weight lifter gradually increases the weights he lifts, and he gradually increases the sets and reps of those weights until his muscles are strong enough to lift the five hundred pounds and he can safely compete. It is the same with us. We have spiritual and emotional muscles that God is growing. There are things in our lives he wants us to prepare for our blessings. So, even in the seasons of waiting, keep learning, keep doing the next right thing, keep growing yourself and following your passions, keep creating. God is working even when we don't see it, and we need to prepare ourselves and our lives for the blessings we have been praying for. We need to wait with anticipation and excitement.

Reference Verses

Genesis 16:1-2

Now Sarai, Abram's wife, had not been able to bear children for him. But she had an Egyptian servant named Hagar. So Sarai said to Abram, "The Lord has prevented me from having children. Go and sleep with my servant. Perhaps I can have children through her." And Abram agreed with Sarai's proposal.

Genesis 17:2-4

"I will make a covenant with you, by which I will guarantee to give you countless descendants." At this, Abram fell face down on the ground. Then God said to him, "This is my covenant with you: I will make you the father of a multitude of nations!"

Genesis 17:17

Then Abraham bowed down to the ground, but he laughed to himself in disbelief. "How could I become a father at the age of 100?" he thought. "And how can Sarah have a baby when she is ninety years old?" So Abraham said to God, "May Ishmael live under your special blessing!" But God replied, "No—Sarah, your wife, will give birth to a son for you. You will name him Isaac, and I will confirm my covenant with him and his descendants as an everlasting covenant."

Genesis 18:14

Is anything too hard for the Lord? I will return about this time next year, and Sarah will have a son."

Genesis 21:2

She became pregnant, and she gave birth to a son for Abraham in his old age. This happened at just the time God had said it would.

Habakkuk 2:3

This vision is for a future time. It describes the end, and it will be fulfilled. If it seems slow in coming, wait patiently, for it will surely take place. It will not be delayed.

Isaiah 40:30-31

Even youths will become weak and tired, and young men will fall in exhaustion. But those who trust in the Lord will find new strength. They will soar high on wings like eagles. They will run and not grow weary. They will walk and not faint.

Lamentations 3:25-26
The Lord is good to those who depend on him, to those who search for him. So it is good to wait quietly for salvation from the Lord.

Micah 7:7
As for me, I look to the Lord for help. I wait confidently for God to save me, and my God will certainly hear me.

Psalm 27:14
Wait patiently for the Lord. Be brave and courageous. Yes, wait patiently for the Lord.

Psalm 75:1-3
We thank you, O God! We give thanks because you are near. People everywhere tell of your wonderful deeds. God says, "At the time I have planned, I will bring justice against the wicked. When the earth quakes and its people live in turmoil, I am the one who keeps its foundations firm."

Ecclesiastes 3:1
For everything there is a season, a time for every activity under heaven.

Ecclesiastes 3:11
Yet God has made everything beautiful for its own time. He has planted eternity in the human heart, but even so, people cannot see the whole scope of God's work from beginning to end.

Acts 1:6-7

So when the apostles were with Jesus, they kept asking him, "Lord, has the time come for you to free Israel and restore our kingdom?" He replied, "The Father alone has the authority to set those dates and times, and they are not for you to know."

Galatians 6:9

So let's not get tired of doing what is good. At just the right time we will reap a harvest of blessing if we don't give up.

2 Peter 3:8-9

But you must not forget this one thing, dear friends: A day is like a thousand years to the Lord, and a thousand years is like a day. The Lord isn't really being slow about his promise, as some people think. No, he is being patient for your sake. He does not want anyone to be destroyed, but wants everyone to repent.

Romans 5:3-6

We can rejoice, too, when we run into problems and trials, for we know that they help us develop endurance. And endurance develops strength of character, and character strengthens our confident hope of salvation. And this hope will not lead to disappointment. For we know how dearly God loves us, because he has given us the Holy Spirit to fill our hearts with his love. When we were utterly helpless, Christ came at just the right time and died for us sinners.

Matthew 14:29

"Yes, come," Jesus said. So Peter went over the side of the boat and walked on the water toward Jesus. But when he saw the strong wind and the waves, he was terrified and began to sink. "Save me, Lord!" he shouted. Jesus immediately reached out and grabbed him. "You have so little faith," Jesus said. "Why do you doubt me?"

Matthew 17:20
"You don't have enough faith," Jesus told them. "I tell you the truth, if you had faith even as small as a mustard seed, you could say to this mountain, 'Move from here to there,' and it would move. Nothing would be impossible."

Romans 8:24-28
We were given this hope when we were saved. (If we already have something, we don't need to hope for it. But if we look forward to something we don't yet have, we must wait patiently and confidently.) And the Holy Spirit helps us in our weakness. For example, we don't know what God wants us to pray for. But the Holy Spirit prays for us with groanings that cannot be expressed in words. And the Father who knows all hearts knows what the Spirit is saying, for the Spirit pleads for us believers in harmony with God's own will. And we know that God causes everything to work together for the good of those who love God and are called according to his purpose for them.

Journal Space

_____

_____

_____

_____

_____

_____

Day 29:

The Boat

Have you ever noticed how, every year, time seems to speed up? Before you know it, a year feels like a month, a month feels like a day. Life goes by so fast that it can feel like we are getting behind. Like somehow, in the speed, we've missed our chance to hop on the boat and accomplish our dreams and goals. Maybe we feel like we are too old to reach our career goals, because we have to compete with younger people who still have more longevity ahead of them. Perhaps it's personal goals we feel are passing us by or have an expiration date. We may desperately want children and fear that we are getting old and our time is almost up. Or maybe it's a relationship that needs reconciling, and we've been so caught up in the busyness of life that what once would have been a simple apology now seems like a huge rift as so much time has gone by without a word. There are moments in life when it feels like we are sitting on the shore, watching our ship sail away without us, feeling helpless as it drifts off into the distance. But at times when we see our boat drifting off without us onboard, this is what God wants us to remember: It doesn't matter if you missed the boat. Our God walks on water, and he has enabled us to do the same.

Life is full of natural circumstances and natural resources, but we were made by and live for a supernatural God—a God of love, and restoration, and redemption, a God whose timing is not our timing and whose ways are not our ways. We are cared for and guided by a God of miracles, who makes the impossible possible. So, the next time that you feel like you have missed the boat, and you see it drifting off into the distance, lift your eyes up above your circumstances to God. Lift your eyes to the one who makes us walk on water and walk fearlessly toward your dreams. Those desires that God placed in your heart and encouraged to grow? He will finish and complete what he started.

Reference Verses

Genesis 21:2-7
She became pregnant, and she gave birth to a son for Abraham in his old age. This happened at just the time God had said it would. And Abraham named their son Isaac. Eight days after Isaac was born, Abraham circumcised him as God had commanded. Abraham was 100 years old when Isaac was born. And Sarah declared, "God has brought me laughter. All who hear about this will laugh with me. Who would have said to Abraham that Sarah would nurse a baby? Yet I have given Abraham a son in his old age!"

Genesis 17:15-17
Then God said to Abraham, "Regarding Sarai, your wife—her name will no longer be Sarai. From now on her name will be Sarah. And I will bless her and give you a son from her! Yes, I will bless her richly, and she will become the mother of many nations. Kings of nations will be among her descendants." Then Abraham bowed down to the ground, but he laughed to himself in disbelief. "How could I become a father at

the age of 100?" he thought. "And how can Sarah have a baby when she is ninety years old?"

Exodus 14:13-22 NKJV

And Moses said to the people, "Do not be afraid. Stand still, and see the salvation of the Lord, which He will accomplish for you today. For the Egyptians whom you see today, you shall see again no more forever. The Lord will fight for you, and you shall hold your peace." And the Lord said to Moses, "Why do you cry to Me? Tell the children of Israel to go forward. But lift up your rod, and stretch out your hand over the sea and divide it. And the children of Israel shall go on dry *ground* through the midst of the sea. And I indeed will harden the hearts of the Egyptians, and they shall follow them. So I will gain honor over Pharaoh and over all his army, his chariots, and his horsemen. Then the Egyptians shall know that I *am* the Lord, when I have gained honor for Myself over Pharaoh, his chariots, and his horsemen." And the Angel of God, who went before the camp of Israel, moved and went behind them; and the pillar of cloud went from before them and stood behind them. So it came between the camp of the Egyptians and the camp of Israel. Thus it was a cloud and darkness *to the one,* and it gave light by night *to the other,* so that the one did not come near the other all that night. Then Moses stretched out his hand over the sea; and the Lord caused the sea to go *back* by a strong east wind all that night, and made the sea into dry *land,* and the waters were divided. So the children of Israel went into the midst of the sea on the dry *ground,* and the waters *were* a wall to them on their right hand and on their left.

Ecclesiastes 3:11

Yet God has made everything beautiful for its own time. He has planted eternity in the human heart, but even so, people cannot see the whole scope of God's work from beginning to end.

Ecclesiastes 8:6

Those who obey him will not be punished. Those who are wise will find a time and a way to do what is right, for there is a time and a way for everything, even when a person is in trouble.

Proverbs 3:5-6 ESV

Trust in the Lord with all your heart, and do not lean on your own understanding. In all your ways acknowledge him, and he will make straight your paths.

Psalm 37:3-4

Trust in the Lord and do good. Then you will live safely in the land and prosper. Take delight in the Lord, and he will give you your heart's desires.

Matthew 14:24-29

Meanwhile, the disciples were in trouble far away from land, for a strong wind had risen, and they were fighting heavy waves. About three o'clock in the morning Jesus came toward them, walking on the water. When the disciples saw him walking on the water, they were terrified. In their fear, they cried out, "It's a ghost!" But Jesus spoke to them at once. "Don't be afraid," he said. "Take courage. I am here!" Then Peter called to him, "Lord, if it's really you, tell me to come to you, walking on the water." "Yes, come," Jesus said. So Peter went over the side of the boat and walked on the water toward Jesus.

Galatians 6:9 ESV

So let's not get tired of doing what is good. At just the right time we will reap a harvest of blessing if we don't give up.

Luke 18:27 ESV
But he said, "What is impossible with man is possible with God."

2 Peter 3:8-9 ESV
But do not overlook this one fact, beloved, that with the Lord one day is as a thousand years, and a thousand years as one day. The Lord is not slow to fulfill his promise as some count slowness, but is patient toward you, not wishing that any should perish, but that all should reach repentance

Journal Space

_____

_____

_____

_____

_____

_____

Day 30:

Remembering the Breakthroughs

How many of us have felt down or disappointed because our lives just weren't where we wanted them to be yet? There are things that we've longed for that haven't come to fruition yet. Things we have fought for and worked tirelessly for that haven't seen their full development yet. Maybe we made huge progress, then felt like we got knocked backwards again. This could be in anything in life: relationships, finances, career goals, any dream. Why do we have these feelings? Because we are our own worst enemies and critics.

There are milestones and time markers that come and go and make us look at life, examining where we are and how far we still want to go. Things like birthdays and holidays are dangerous for the mind in this way because it's so easy to see time passing, to realize that another year has come and gone and we're still not where we wanted to be. How easy it is for us to forget how far we've come. How easy it is for us to forget what we've accomplished, what healing we've come through, and how we've grown as people. We look at forward progression, and when we feel like we are stagnant, or maybe like we've been knocked backwards, we tend to forget the breakthroughs along the way.

We forget that all the little things that we do matter. Those choices we make every day, to work on something we care about, even for just ten minutes. The call we make to a friend to reach out and share what's on our hearts that brings us closer. The way we touch people along our journey. We forget that everything we do matters. It doesn't matter if this life knocks us backward sometimes, it doesn't take away those breakthroughs.

It may feel like we've lost ground at times, but the work we put in along the way matters—our accomplishments matter. Our willingness to show up and be vulnerable matters. Those are the seeds we've planted along the way that are preparing a future harvest for us. We can't see seeds as they sprout underground. We can't see them as they are battered by rain, but they sprout and grow nevertheless. So, we may not be where we want to be yet but thank God we are not where we were. It is a constant pressing on and forward progression, and we all have to remember that even in those moments when we feel like we are stagnant, or backsliding, what we do still matters and what we've done still counts. This life isn't just about the destination; it's about the journey.

Reference Verses

Deuteronomy 6:12
Be careful not to forget the Lord, who rescued you from slavery in the land of Egypt.

Lamentations 3:22-23
The faithful love of the Lord never ends! His mercies never cease. Great is his faithfulness; his mercies begin afresh each morning.

1 Samuel 12:24
But be sure to fear the Lord and faithfully serve him. Think of all the wonderful things he has done for you.

Psalm 77:10-11
And I said, "This is my fate; the Most High has turned his hand against me." But then I recall all you have done, O Lord; I remember your wonderful deeds of long ago. They are constantly in my thoughts. I cannot stop thinking about your mighty works.

Psalm 143:4-6
I am losing all hope; I am paralyzed with fear. I remember the days of old. I ponder all your great works and think about what you have done. I lift my hands to you in prayer. I thirst for you as parched land thirsts for rain.

Psalm 103:2
Let all that I am praise the Lord; may I never forget the good things he does for me.

Psalm 106:7-8
Our ancestors in Egypt were not impressed by the Lord's miraculous deeds. They soon forgot his many acts of kindness to them. Instead, they rebelled against him at the Red Sea. Even so, he saved them to defend the honor of his name and to demonstrate his mighty power.

Psalm 126:6 GNT
Those who wept as they went out carrying seed will come back singing for joy, as they bring in the harvest.

Psalm 105:5

Remember the wonders he has performed, his miracles, and the rulings he has given

Galatians 6:9 ESV

And let us not grow weary of doing good, for in due season we will reap, if we do not give up.

Mark 4:26-27

Jesus also said, "The Kingdom of God is like a farmer who scatters seed on the ground. Night and day, while he's asleep or awake, the seed sprouts and grows, but he does not understand how it happens."

Matthew 7:7

Keep on asking, and you will receive what you ask for. Keep on seeking, and you will find. Keep on knocking, and the door will be opened to you.

Romans 4:20-24

Abraham never wavered in believing God's promise. In fact, his faith grew stronger, and in this he brought glory to God. He was fully convinced that God is able to do whatever he promises. And because of Abraham's faith, God counted him as righteous. And when God counted him as righteous, it wasn't just for Abraham's benefit. It was recorded for our benefit, too, assuring us that God will also count us as righteous if we believe in him, the one who raised Jesus our Lord from the dead.

Philippians 1:6

And I am certain that God, who began the good work within you, will continue his work until it is finally finished on the day when Christ Jesus returns.

Journal Space

_____

_____

_____

_____

_____

_____

Conclusion

I hope that in reading this devotional, you've come to know how deeply loved you are by God. "God loves us deeply. He is full of mercy." (Eph. 2:4 NIRV). I hope you know that you are seen, heard, and known by God. "The eyes of the Lord watch over those who do right, and his ears are open to their prayers" (1 Peter 3:12). I hope you know that God created you to be uniquely you, and that who you are matters to Him. "For you created my inmost being; you knit me together in my mother's womb." (Psalm 139:13 NIV). Nothing is hidden from God—not the thoughts in your mind, the doubts in your heart, or your worst deeds—and yet, you are still precious to Him. "Nothing in all creation is hidden from God. Everything is naked and exposed before his eyes, and he is the one to whom we are accountable." (Hebrews 4:13) I hope you know that it is never God's will for you to be mistreated, or to stay in a place or with people where you are being abused. As the Scriptures say, "You must remove the evil person from among you" (1 Cor. 5:13). I hope you've come to know that your desires, wants, needs, and happiness matter to God, and that He has good plans for your life. "Take delight in the Lord, and he will give you your heart's desires" (Psalm 37:4). I hope you have come to believe again that anything is possible with God (Matthew 19:26). I hope that this devotional is just a part of your journey digging deeper into God's love. And, I hope that you find a community to share healing with others and maybe even go through this devotional together.

Acknowledgements

To Morgan James Publishing, thank you for believing in this book, its message, and its power to provide hope and healing for people.

To the friends and acquaintances who connected me with Morgan James, especially Jim Paar.

To my friends and family, thank you for encouraging me, reading, and listening to the devotionals as I wrote them and for believing in the book.

To my counselor, Abbe Utter, thank you for helping me to heal enough to be able to write a book to help others find victory and healing.

Thank You Gift!

Thank you for reading my book! Writing this book was a journey, that started with my song, "Believe Again." I wrote this song on a day when I was having a rough PTSD trigger, and I was feeling like I'd been run over by a train emotionally. I wanted to write truthfully about the process of healing and bring hope into that process. This song comforted my heart so much through my healing, and I want to share it with you as a gift. I hope it brings comfort to you in your process as well!

Get your FREE download of Brittany's song "Believe Again" by going to:
www.Believeagain.club

Find more music and books from Brittany Bexton at:
www.BrittanyBexton.com
www.Learningtobelieveagain.com

About the Author

Brittany Bexton grew up along the California coast and attended the Pacific Conservatory Theater (PCPA), where she studied acting, singing, and dancing. After doing professional theater for years, she decided it was time to pursue her own music more fully, and began focusing on her own songwriting and performances, along with doing film, TV, and print work. In 2011, Brittany Moved to Nashville, Tennessee to pursue her music full-time. Since moving to Nashville, Brittany has released two albums, with a third on the way, toured in 18 states, made TV and radio appearances, and had her music featured on both terrestrial, and online radio stations throughout the US, Europe, Canada, and Australia.

CPSIA information can be obtained
at www.ICGtesting.com
Printed in the USA
BVHW031931220120
570167BV00014B/33